Teaching the Child Under Six

. . . a personal and practical approach
to early education in nursery schools,
kindergartens, day care centers, church
schools, and community action programs
in Merrill's

Early Childhood Education Series
under the editorship of
James L. Hymes, Jr.

...by the author

other books...

Before The Child Reads
Behavior and Misbehavior
Being A Good Parent
A Child Development Point of View
The Child Under Six
Discipline
Effective Home-School Relations
Understanding Your Child

for children...

Books To Start On
Books To Stretch On

with Lucia Manley Hymes...

Hooray for Chocolate
Oodles of Noodles

Teaching the Child Under Six

James L. Hymes, Jr.
University of Maryland

Charles E. Merrill Publishing Company
Columbus, Ohio
A Bell & Howell Company

Preface

Built into this book are two long-cherished hopes.

The first: that the day will soon come when all young children will have the chance to begin their schooling in "first grade" — and this first grade will be for three-year-olds. Fours will go to second grade, five-year-olds to third grade.

Gone will be the special names: nursery school, kindergarten, day care . . . . Gone the special programs born of emergencies: Head Start, Title I . . . . Gone the tuition charges limiting early education to the few.

Instead, hopefully, public education will be free and available to every child from age three on, for whatever length of day or year and with whatever services the child's needs or his family's needs require. Surely soon what we now call "first" must become fourth grade. The school which does not serve its three-, four-, and five-year-olds must be seen as incomplete, unfinished — strangely, oddly beginning in the middle.

The second hope: that we will serve our young children well. No one gains if more boys and girls come to school but their schooling turns out to be wrong for their age. The expansion of public early education can mean a new, exciting chance to build programs of the highest quality, delicately in tune with children's nature and with our nation's style, yet consistent with good scholarship.

These hopes center on three-, four-, and five-year-olds, and on their school life. This specific focus is not meant to minimize the importance of those years which should be called the "preschool" years: from birth to age three. Nor to minimize the importance of each child's education within his home, by his basic teachers — his parents.

But two hopes are enough for one book, especially two of such fundamental importance to children and to all of us.

James L. Hymes, Jr.

College Park, Maryland
April 1968

Table of Contents

1

The State of the Profession

Early education occurs under many names: nursery school, kindergarten, day care center, Head Start.... The variety of names makes it sound as if each program were drastically different from all the others. This is not true.

There are administrative and organizational differences, but none of these is very important so far as teaching the children is concerned. Day care children, Head Start children, nursery school children, kindergarten children are ... children! And they have one bond in common: They are *young* children. The education of all of them ought to be basically the same. *Once a child is in the group the similarities overwhelmingly should outweigh the differences.* The name of their group should no longer matter.

If you were to visit a group in the middle of the morning you ought not to be able to tell by looking at the equipment or the program or the teaching methods: Is this a nursery school? A day care center? A Head Start group? Unless you were very skilled in judging children's ages you ought not to be able to tell: Is this a nursery school? A kindergarten?

1

If you were to visit a group in the late afternoon you could make a good guess: This is probably a day care center. But you shouldn't be able to tell by looking at the teacher or the materials or the activity. You would guess by looking at the clock. Day care centers are the only programs operating at that time.

The basic educational equipment, supplies, and materials ought to be the same — nursery school or kindergarten or day care or Head Start. The space requirements should be about the same. The adult-child ratio and the standards for class size ought to be similar. The tone and spirit of the group, the methods of teaching, the content ought to be the same.

This basic similarity should carry over to the Sabbath. Probably the very largest number of young children have their first experience in education outside the home in church schools. These are brief experiences, only a few hours one day a week. The content taught in these schools sometimes — not always — differs from the content of general education. Yet young children are still young children on the Sabbath. The methods of teaching, the climate of their groups, the class size and the adult-child ratio, the materials and equipment ought to be geared to the age. Religious education, church-sponsored, often finds itself freed from the critical thinking and legal regulations that control general education. Churches have the leeway to do whatever they want to do, because they do it in the name of religion. And for that very reason — because it is done in the name of religion — they want their early education to be the very best. It is hoped that much that follows in this book will help these churches make their Sabbath experiences for young children exactly that: As good and as right for the age as they can possibly be.

THE IMMEDIATE GOAL

Most important: Once a child is in the group, the immediate goal of all the programs — nursery school and kindergarten and day care and Head Start, even Sunday School — should be the same. The name of the group should not make any difference.

These are schools, all of them; they are not "pre" schools. These are schools for general education; they are not "prep" schools.

Neither are they technical or quasi-trade schools for teaching some one specific skill.

These are schools for the development of the whole child. Each of them — nursery school, kindergarten, day care, Head Start — helps children develop to the maximum their intellectual powers, their social powers, their emotional capacities, their physical powers.

Why have nursery schools? Why kindergartens? Why Head Start? What will a child gain in a day care center? The common aim of all the groups is to help children learn, and to do it in such a way that the youngsters live their years of ages three and four and five in the richest, most satisfying, most constructive manner possible. The one big job of all the groups, once a child is enrolled, is *to teach* so that each youngster is more glad he is alive during these early years.

FUTURE PAYOFFS

Nursery school, kindergarten, day care, Head Start are schools for *now*. Their eyes are steadfastly on the present. But good early education almost always pays an extra dividend: It pays off in the future, too. This is the bonus.

Sound programs provide experiences in literature and music and art, in the sciences and in mathematics, in the social sciences. They provide experiences in health and in physical education. Children have the chance to gain in language, to expand their store of knowledge, to grow in curiosity and in problem-solving and in creativity, to stretch their attention spans. Youngsters have the chance to improve in coordination, balance, speed, grace, vigor, strength. They have the chance to widen their sense of trust in adults and to deepen their sense of joy in their age-mates. They have the chance to grow in independence, in self-direction and in self-control. Sound programs are thoughtfully oriented to our democratic values. Children have the chance to live in a little plot of American society operating at its very best.

No guarantees come with all of this. Early education can only promise to help make the third and fourth and fifth years of life good ones. It cannot insure without fail that any tomorrow will be successful. Nothing "fixes" a child for life, no matter what happens next. *But!* Exciting, pleasing early experiences are seldom sloughed off. They go with the child, on into first grade, on into the child's long life ahead.

Exciting, pleasing early experiences have a special significance, too. Folk wisdom, as well as modern psychology, tells us what it is: As the twig is bent ... From little acorns ... A stitch in time ... The child's experiences in nursery school, kindergarten, day care, Head Start are his foundational experiences, his initial relationships, the beginnings. These first impressions have a unique, predisposing importance.

The child is lucky — we all are lucky — when good early education gets him off to a strong start. Lucky the child who finds his first schooling rewarding. Lucky the child who is not a reluctant adventurer, regretfully existing where he is, longingly wishing for where he had been. Moving onward and upward and outward is the story of life. Moving onward and upward and outward with zest and joy is the good life.

PROBLEMS FACING EARLY EDUCATION

People are fond of saying that nursery-kindergarten education is the best, primary education is the next best, and so on up the list until you come to graduate education which allegedly is the worst of all. If there must be gradations, this is as it should be. Early education ought to be very, very good.

Often it is. Sometimes it is not.

Many programs are too pushy. They are too narrow; they hold the wrong goals. They cannot look on their youngsters as three years old or four or five. They see them only as pre-first-graders. The sixth year of life looms on the horizon like a darkening cloud. Early education in these groups is simply boot camp for a forbidding future that lies ahead. It manipulates its children and manages them without respect or sensitivity or decency.

Other classrooms are too passive. They challenge their children too little. They let their youngsters drift and wander. The children in them pass their third or fourth or fifth year of life pleasantly enough, but the children stay on a plateau. They seldom feel fully involved or excited or alive. They seldom get the kick out of their learning and their life that young children should. Good teaching does not push children around; neither does it let them simply fool around.

The most serious problem facing early education, however, is that there simply is not enough of it. We are barely scratching the surface in providing the programs that young children need. We call youngsters under six "preschool" children. They are "pre-school" . . . only because we don't have the schools for them. We don't have enough nursery schools. We don't have enough kinder-gartens. We don't have enough day care centers. We don't have enough Head Start or Title I programs.

We Americans talk about equal educational opportunity. In fact, we practice great discrimination. We practice age discrimi-nation! Children under six are grossly underserved.

America pays lip service to the importance of these early years, but our deeds do not square with our words. We have many more *never-ins* than drop-outs. Far too many of our young children, never in school, live their third or fourth or fifth year of life underemployed, underchallenged, wasting their time, missing the chance to live up to their potential. The severe shortage of pro-grams is the number one problem facing early education. Anyone who cares about young children must work to solve this shortage at all of its levels: nursery education, kindergarten education, day care education, compensatory education. It is not enough for any of us simply to do a good job with our own children within our own little classroom. A good teacher has an allegiance to children — to all of them.

The Shortage of Programs

It is easy to be overimpressed and misled by the recent surge of interest in the education of young children. It is true that there are many upswinging developments. Private nursery schools are mush-rooming. Head Start enrolled about half a million young children in each of its first three summers of operation; it served more than one hundred thousand children in each of its first two year-round sessions. The number of states providing aid for kindergartens is increasing. The number of day care centers is going up.

It gives the impression that we are doing a lot, *but* underneath all the flurry and all the excitement the basic problem facing early education remains: We are still reaching only a handful of our young children.

Only 29 states provide state aid for kindergartens; 21 do not. And most of the 29 provide only *half* aid; that is, 50% of the aid given to children aged six.

Only about 60% of our five-year-olds go to any kind of kindergarten: public, private, church-sponsored. About 40% go to no school at all.

There are approximately 12.5 million children in the three to five age group. It is estimated that 29.4% go to school; 70.6% do not.[1] And this estimate may well be high. In Maryland, one of the more advanced states in nursery education, a private study indicates that approximately 2.5% of the state's four-year-olds go to school; the percentage of three-year-olds in school is infinitesimal.

Not a single state provides state aid for public nursery schools. Three- and four-year-olds pay tuition to go to school. This means that only the lucky children of the wealthier or more conscientious parents have this opportunity.

Public money for the support of day care centers is pitifully small. One state out of fifty, California, provides state aid. New York City and Philadelphia provide local tax support. Federal funds are potentially available through the Children's Bureau, the Bureau of Family Services, the Public Health Service, and the Office of Education — all in the Department of Health, Education and Welfare; especially through the Office of Economic Opportunity; even through the Department of Housing and Urban Development. But the funds are not earmarked for day care, and day care tends to get lost in the shuffle. The available federal money, not large enough to begin with, is not always fully requested by local and state agencies. The result is that the instances of public investment in day care are minor exceptions. For the most part day care is bought by the tuition of families who can least afford to pay tuition or is provided by charity, a most unstable and ungenerous base of support.

---

[1]Statistics from *Nursery-Kindergarten Enrollment of Children Under Six: October 1966*. Washington: U.S. Government Printing Office, 1967.

It has been estimated that only 2% of our working mothers the country over are able to place their children in group care facilities. A detailed study in one city, Baltimore, revealed that only 5% of the children under six needing day care in that city were being served in licensed day care centers.[2] We know how to give young children excellent care when their mothers are not available, but we are not doing it.

The one seemingly impressive figure — 560,000 young children in the first and largest Summer Head Start — is actually cause for shame rather than elation. It is estimated that 1,193,000 young children in each age bracket live in poverty, a total of approximately 3,600,000 at ages three, four, and five. Summer Head Start reached about one-seventh of these youngsters — primarily at one age level — and for a quickie, condensed, eight-week program. We can be pleased but hardly gleeful over this tiny advance.

The minuscule nature of our "advance" is best illustrated in year-round compensatory programs. Year-round Head Start has reached at its peak only 190,000 young children and, because of difficulties in funding, not always for the full school year. Title I funds of the Elementary and Secondary Education Act are used to provide programs for only another 190,000 at the most, and, because of differing standards, not always at the same quality as Head Start.

There have been day nurseries or day care centers in the United States since 1854. We have had kindergartens since 1855. We have had nursery schools since before 1920. Dynamic, progressive, forward-marching America is sometimes stymied by problems whose solutions evade us. But we know what to do about the under-education of young children. We simply aren't doing enough of it. There is only one possible conclusion: The U.S.A. is short-changing children under six. Frighteningly large numbers of children are operating under less than full steam because we have no groups at all to serve them. Especially those young children needing day care services and those needing compensatory education are being positively harmed in the many places where we have no groups at all to serve them.

---

[2]*Report of a Survey of Resident Working Mothers and the Day Care of Their Children in Baltimore City in 1964* (Baltimore, Md., 1965). Division of Child Day Care and Bureau of Biostatistics.

Why Is There a Shortage of Programs?

Gross and widespread misunderstanding about young children is one of the reasons why we invest so little money in their education. Many people — especially those not living with them or near them — still think of children under six as little babies tied to their mother's apron strings. Age six stays pegged in the public's mind as the time when children are ready to learn. A large part of the general public completely underestimates the maturity of three-, four-, and five-year-olds.

The low quality of commercial television programming for young children is a symbol of this misestimate of young children's abilities. It aims almost exclusively at amusement and treats young children as if they were pre-thinking, pre-feeling, tots to be titilated, but not real people with ideas, with taste, with awareness of and interest in the world around them. This point of view underlies our national unwillingness to provide school programs for young children. Too many people persist in thinking: "What could threes and fours and fives possibly learn?"

A second cause of our lack of spending money on schools for the young is our tendency to overrate the home. We blithely assume that good homes can meet all the needs of young children. Worse: We mistakenly assume that all homes are good. We close our eyes to the changes in home life wrought by urbanization and technology. We forget that millions of young children are cooped up in city apartments; that millions live in commuter community suburban areas; that millions of farm children live lonely lives. We prefer not to face up to the fact that 3.7 million mothers of children under six are in the labor force and not home at all. The dream picture — a mother and her young child playing together, talking together, whiling away the happy hours together — clouds our view of reality.

Our confused thinking about what today's home can and cannot do well has slowed the growth of public kindergartens and stymied the development of public nursery schools. Mothers who seek more intellectual and social and physical stimulation for their children than they, alone in their homes, are able to provide are made to feel that they are trying to get rid of their youngsters. This confusion has especially frustrated the development of good day care services. We seem to be afraid that the availability of day care will make it too easy for women to work. We are not sufficiently alarmed by how the absence of good day care complicates the lot of the women who must work and who have always worked, and how it harms their children. We won't let ourselves think of a system of guidance and counselling, helping women to stay at home who really want to do that, helping those who must work or want to work to do their work with peace of mind, knowing their children are cared for well.

Our country's economic situation is another reason why there is a shortage of programs for young children. We are the world's richest country, possibly the richest country since the beginning of time. Potentially we have the wealth to do anything and everything that young children's needs require; but at the same time we are "poor." Because of our past wars, ever-present wars, and preparations for future wars, we spend so large a share of our vast resources on defense budgeting that there is not enough money left for the expansion of education, or for the needed public and social services. Humanitarian and educational efforts in the United States lag far behind our needs.

The frightful expense of war makes the education of young children scramble with all other levels of education for the remnants of funds left in the public purse. With not enough money to go around, the growth of under-six education competes with the growth of higher education, with the equally needed expansion of junior colleges and community colleges and universities. It competes with elementary and secondary education. Unfortunately, under-six education — the newer field — loses out. Until we Americans make wiser decisions on how to spend our vast wealth the expansion of under-six education will come painfully slowly.

Some day Americans must take the pledge: *We want top-quality public education for all young children.* We want public programs of highest quality for whatever duration of day or week or year the child or the family's needs require.

We must have public nursery schools for three- and four-year-olds.

We must have public kindergartens for five-year-olds.

We must have whatever supplementary and compensatory programs may be needed, enough so they are available to every young child who needs them, available early enough in development to be effective, available in sufficient duration to be effective, and topnotch in quality.

The Urgent Need for Day Care

We must have public day care centers — this is an especially urgent need. The young children whose mothers cannot be at home with them are our most vulnerable young children. We must have public day care centers that hold sound goals — the same goals as good nursery schools and good kindergartens and good Head Start and Title I programs. We must have public day care centers with the space, materials, equipment, and trained staff to meet these goals. We must have public day care centers with skilled counseling staffs to help mothers think through whether or not they should work and, if they must, whether or not group day care is the best solution for their particular child.

We are very far from accepting the notion that good day care should be available free — just as first grade is, or twelfth grade. Yet our ultimate commitment has to be the same as our public school commitment: To provide whatever service a child or his family needs. We don't charge the fourth grader extra if he requires remedial reading help or speech therapy or individual testing. We try fully to serve each child in terms of his need. Until we build this attitude about day care we may have to settle for some intermediate steps. We ought at least to work for enough public support so that it, plus parent payments on a sliding scale adjusted to income, will guarantee a high quality program. The present basis of support — tuition from working parents, most of them poor, or insufficient aid from community chests or private charity — dooms day care to insufficient programs and programs of meagre quality with overly large groups, improper equipment, untrained staffs.

For a brief period public schools operated day care centers. The Lanham Child Care Centers set up during World War II for the children of war-working mothers were under public school supervision. The bulk of support came from the federal government and this ended when the war ended. Today public schools are not involved in the business. They think of day care as baby-sitting. This is all that many day care centers offer, but none should. Public schools are thrown off by the name *day care,* but names should not matter. Once a child is in the group, no matter why he comes in the first place, the big job is early education — the same job the kindergarten and Head Start and the nursery school do — done the same way but over longer hours.

It would be a great gain if public education would rekindle its sense of responsibility and again operate day care centers. The kind of educational leadership that public education could bring would do much to end the low quality of day care. Whether or not this direct involvement comes soon, public education has an immediate stake in the quality of day care. Many day care children have already led disrupted lives. They spend long hours in their groups, almost all their waking hours. They all eventually become "public school children." They can enter our schools with a backlog of healthy living behind them or, if they must be consigned to low-quality programs or left alone to drift, they will enter doubly damaged — hurt by the strains within their home life and hurt by the lackluster of their early group life.

Pushy Programs

We need more programs; we need to improve the programs we have. Too many existing classrooms for young children have this overriding goal: To get the children ready for first grade. This goal is unworthy. It is hurtful.

This goal has had the most distorting impact on five-year-olds. It causes kindergartens to be merely the handmaidens of first grade. First grade sets the standards, it sets the style. Eyes must be on it. Kindergarten teachers cannot look at their own children and plan for their present needs as five-year-olds.

We say that there ought to be no sharp break between kindergarten and first grade. First graders, after all, are only three months older than they were in June at the end of their five-year-old program. Many first grades, in fact, include large numbers of five-year-olds, children who are 5.9 or 5.10 or even younger. We speak of "articulation" between kindergarten and first grade. We are careful in our terminology to talk of *K* through 6, *K* through 8. We speak of the need to make the transition from a five-year-old program to a first grade program slow, gradual, imperceptible. And we have done it — but how we have done it! More and more kindergartens are like bad first grades; first grades are not becoming like good kindergartens!

The undesirable aspects of first grade often seep down most quickly. Get-them-ready-for-first-grade kindergartens stress "socialization." But too often they equate pre-first-grade socialization with conformity. The main goal is to produce a child who will fit in and not cause any trouble. Walking in line, walking on tiptoes, using "our indoor voices," raising one's hand — these are the overly-prized social skills.

Pre-first-grade socialization too often is equated with obedience. The main goal is to produce a child who will mind and do what his teacher tells him (and, in the process, begin to learn to do what anyone "in authority" says: boss, corporal, leader . . .). The basis for the morality is watching the other fellow. The ultimate reason for doing or not doing something is that "WE" do or don't do it: "WE don't throw sand" . . . "WE don't shout" . . . "WE wait our turn."

Pre-first-grade socialization too often is equated with erasing individuality. The fully socialized five-year-old is an in-member of the group. He finishes his work when the group finishes. He comes to every Story Time. He is musical when it is Music Time and arty because it is Art Time. He turns on imagination and creativity because it is time to act out "Little Red Riding Hood" or "Billy Goats Gruff."

The picture is no more cheering on the academic side. Routinizing procedures are imported: Show-and-Tell . . . workbooks . . . coloring . . . Good Morning songs . . . dreary nose-counting attendance taking . . . too much teacher-talk while shushed children sit in a circle. Dullest content is borrowed: a heavy-handed harping on *up, down, left, right* . . . even a fussing with phonics. It sometimes seems as if those parts of first grade least right for six-year-olds are the ones most apt to be imposed on fives.

So much that is wrong for children under six is done in the name of Reading Readiness. "Readiness" is talked about as if it were a distinct and scholarly field of study, like physics or history or literature, but a field especially designed for kindergarten children. If this were true, it would be a sad mistake because the content of this so-called field is dishwatery and anti-intellectual; many of its methods — contrived sets of paper-and-pencil puzzles

— are drab and artificial. Good kindergartens teach reading to their children, as much as the children are ready for. They teach reading in lively, functional ways that their five-year-olds are ready for. They stay far away from the made-up readiness gimmicks.

Kindergarten must get rid of the pressure of preparing children for first grade. First grades can find their own good goals and their own good ways of proceeding in light of the children who enter first grade. Kindergarten has its legitimate job to do.

The "Dribble-down Disease"

This awe and dread of first grade is beginning to stain the nursery school. *Its* job is to get children ready for kindergarten.

Some day care centers, worried about first grade, deny their own educational significance — they send their five-year-olds away from their own program in the morning so that the children can be sure to get the readiness program of a public school kindergarten. Other day care centers mimic what they think a kindergarten ought to do. They give their five-year-olds lessons on learning the alphabet, learning the colors, learning to count to 10.

The impending onslaught of first grade can have an especially corrosive effect on Head Start and Title I programs. The corrosion goes on despite the clear and sound official position of Head Start. Head Start is deeply concerned with later school success but it recognizes that many human qualities feed into success: the child's confidence in himself, his trust in adults, his motivation to learn, his background of success, his ease with his age-mates. Head Start calls its groups Child Development Centers. It envisages them as centers for the whole child — for his physical and social and emotional and intellectual development — and as centers for the family from which that child comes and for the neighborhood in which that family has its roots.

In the official Head Start view, a child's success in first grade and in his long life ahead is not dependent on the forced mastery of a few tiny readiness tricks. Head Start is concerned with its children living their Head Start time vigorously and healthfully in ways that are right for the children at that time.

There is many a slip twixt the cup and the lip, however. Some compensatory programs zero in on readiness activities with a fervor fiercer even than that of the frightened kindergarten. The shortage of skilled teachers of young children is one reason for this excess of zeal. The quantity and promotion of readiness materials is another reason. The terrible time-panic that can engulf Head Start and other compensatory programs is another grave source of pressure.

No professional in early education ever thought that the short weeks of Summer Head Start could work miracles in making up for all the deprivations that four or five years of poverty living had caused. Even the longer period of year-round Head Start, thus far the privilege of very few poor children, cannot in itself compensate for three or four times that span of earlier deprivation. Youngsters who have been hurt by the bleakness and isolation of poverty need a long stretch of years, all organized with the special interests and capacities and enthusiasms of these particular children in mind. But when first grade is seen as the end of time, Head Start teachers lose all freedom to plan for their children during this fourth or fifth year of their life.

> Teaching Disadvantaged Children in the Preschool, *by Carl Bereiter and Siegfried Engelmann (Englewood Cliffs, N.J.: Prentice-Hall, Inc., 1966) is the best book to read to appreciate how devastating a program for young children of the poor can be, once first grade time-panic sets in.*

This kowtowing to first grade — in kindergarten, in Head Start, in nursery school, in day care — is an insult to first grade teachers. They need no one to soften up the children for them or to break the children in. Good first grade teachers can do their job. They have the same job every teacher faces: To work with the children who come. And the hegemony of first grade is an insult to teachers of children under six. We are professionals and we have our work cut out for us: To teach the children who come to us, the children who are now three or four or five.

Developmental Theory

This "dribble-down disease" is an old one. The education of children under six is not the only level to suffer from it. High schools have long paid a price because they must get their youngsters ready for college. The junior high school feels it has to get its boys and girls ready for high school. Fifth and sixth grades know the cold shadow of junior high school. Even the first grade teacher has her eye on second grade and imposes its standards on her six-year-olds.

Developmental theory describes an upward-moving process. Children carry much of their infancy with them into toddlerhood; they carry much of their toddler nature on into years three and four and five; many of their under-six characteristics stay with them as they move on into later childhood. Developmental theory envisages an emerging self, slowly opening up, expanding, tentatively reaching out into new and higher forms of behavior.

Incorrect educational practice is the reverse, a downward-moving process. Tomorrow's schooling shapes today's. A recent comic strip wasn't very comical when it pictured a five-year-old, not feeling well, who didn't dare stay home from kindergarten: "I don't want to miss getting into the college of my choice."

An effort to break this top-heavy power structure was made in the late 1930's. The Commission on the Relation of School and College of the Progressive Education Association worked out arrangements so that the graduates of thirty high schools could be admitted to college on their principals' recommendations, rather than on the basis of having followed a rigid college preparatory program. The thirty schools were freed to develop curricula tuned to the needs of their high school youth on the premise that college in its turn could take care of itself.[3]

The thirty high schools, free agents by agreement, did not all take equal advantage of their release from existing academic pressure. Some schools did freely experiment, however. The results were exactly as developmental theory would lead one to expect. The more that high schools developed programs which were "right" at that time for their adolescents, the better those students succeeded in college. The same will hold true for under-six education: The more fully we meet the needs of our children — *now*, when they are with us, as three-, four-, five-year-olds — the more effectively the children will meet whatever demands are put on them in their tomorrows.

Psychiatric experience provides strong support for this confidence. Those who crumple under life's later demands — the

---

[3]*Adventure in American Education* (New York: Harper and Row, Publishers, 1942, 5 volumes).

pressures of marriage, the pressures of war, the pressure of independent existence — do so usually because their earlier life experiences were unsatisfactory. Good early living is no sure guarantee
of strength and stability as life moves along. Later trauma can be
so overpowering that, no matter how supportive early childhood
was, life confronts man with more than he can stand. But good
early experiences strengthen the human, they do not weaken him.
In reverse, unsatisfactory early experiences weaken the human,
they do not prepare him.

Cognitive Development

The long-standing exploitation of early education for getting
children ready for first grade has received massive reenforcement
from the "knowledge explosion." This is a post World War II
phenomenon. Russia's space achievements sharpened our awareness of it. Our own space progress and our advances in every area
— medicine, communication, transportation, food production, pro-
cessing — all have centered our attention on the need for knowledge. America has a frightened sense that there is so much to
know today, so much to find out, so little time to do it in.

At older age levels the knowledge explosion has led to burgeoning
enrollments in colleges. In under-six education it has meant: You
can't start too early — learn, learn, learn! Cognitive development
has become the status symbol of much early education.

Cognitive development is, of course, a legitimate concern in the
education of children under six. The new bright spotlight on it can
be a very useful prod to those schools that err by having programs
that are too passive. In many programs, however, cognitive development has become the sole concern.

The need for children with more knowledge is not the only need
our recent past has uncovered. We need children with better feelings and sounder social sensitivities fully as much. Education
makes a major error when it concentrates on knowledge alone.

The error is compounded when cognitive development is equated
with the old readiness devices, with constant talking at children,
with artificial lessons unrelated to children's living. Some of the
"newest" ideas in the recent surge for cognitive development are
identical with the approaches in old workbooks: "The goal of this
exercise is to teach the names of shapes (circle, square, triangle,

rectangle) . . . to teach the colors (red, blue, green, yellow, black, brown) . . . to teach concepts (under, on top of, over, beside, small, larger) . . . to teach counting (1, 2, 3, 4)." The battle cry is new but the result is old: We bring the dreary parts of first grade down into younger children's lives.

Children under six must use their minds, and they want to. They must learn, and they want to. But the challenge to good education is to find the content and the methods of teaching that fit the young child. Then his mind will really stretch. A youngster is not necessarily thinking his best because he is sitting his straightest. The particular challenge is to find the ways of teaching that are most apt to encourage a child to go on with learning. There *is* so much to learn today, more than the pushiest program can ever cram into children no matter how early it starts. Our concern has to be to develop a love of learning. Because of the knowledge explosion children will have to continue learning, on their own, all through their lives.

Passive Programs

Passive programs are almost as hurtful as pushy ones. Passive programs are monuments to missed teaching opportunities.

Custodial Care

For years in the past most day care centers had too passive a program. Too many still do even today. The goal of old-time day care was simply to provide custodial care: to take the child, to keep him safe, to return him whole to his parent at the end of the day, in one piece and undamaged.

The millions of mothers of young children who are working today or who cannot care for their children at home because of illness or some other reason can understand this simple goal. The pressures on these mothers are such that, if need be, they will gladly settle for someone who will keep their child out of harm's way. They are willing, often desperate, to buy such a program if they can afford it.

There is nothing wrong with the word "care." The education of young children is the education of dependent children, of active children, the education of youngsters with little impulse control and little understanding of potential dangers. Children under six, more than any other age, are prone to accidental death and injury. *Good* care is a legitimate concern of every group: nursery school, kindergarten, Head Start, and day care. Every good teacher in every good program, no matter what its name, owes it to a parent to say: "I will be responsible . . . I, the teacher, am here; you, the mother, are not . . . I will do whatever needs doing, just as you would if you could; you can rest assured."

We can meet well this minimum standard: comforting young children, as a good mother would, when they need comfort; listening, as a good mother would; being thrilled with achievement, as a good mother would; feeding when a child is hungry; letting the sleepy child sleep; individualizing and personalizing, as a good mother would. Good care — nurturing, protecting — is so rock-bottom a goal that we often forget to spell it out and sometimes forget to provide it.

Custodial care is something different, however. A custodial care center is like a parking lot. Presumably you get your child back in the same condition in which you left him: no dented fenders, no paint scraped, no changes for the worse, and none for the better, either. Nurses in sterile white caps and uniforms often were in charge of early day care centers. Their job was to keep the children from doing anything, because doing something might lead to trouble. Today the nurses have disappeared; in their place are minimally trained staffs. Custodial care demands little skill or insight. No one is supposed to teach the child anything; the job is primarily to keep an eye on him. Custodial care demands little equipment or materials or supplies. Only one big expenditure seems legitimate: a television set. It keeps the children quiet.

The goal is narrow. The goal is unrealistic.

Young children share a characteristic with all ages: *They learn from everything and they learn all the time.* They learn from what we set out to teach them; they learn also when no one thinks a lesson is being taught. There are direct learnings *and* there are incidental learnings. Children never come, stay, go, untouched by an experience, experiencing no change for the worse and none for the better.

In custodial care the unsuspected side-effects can be disastrous. No one sets out to teach it, but there is the danger that children will learn passivity: Don't show initiative, they will yell at you . . . Don't be curious, it gets you into trouble . . . Don't ask questions, no one listens.

No one sets out to teach it, but there is the danger that children will learn conformity: Don't get out of line, that leads to difficulty. There is the danger that they will learn not to trust adults and not to trust themselves. Children dropped at a custodial care center, herded at a custodial care center, ignored at a custodial care center may learn ways of rebellion or ways of escape.

Custodial care centers often deny that they are teaching anything. They do this to avoid having to meet standards for staff, equipment, space, program that are set for schools. Many state departments of education are foolishly reluctant to license day care centers. They say: "These are not schools" and gladly relinquish the job of supervision to the department of health or welfare. Saying "We are not teaching anything" and "These are not schools" does not alter the fact. It simply gives custodial centers the freedom to be bad schools.

The inescapable fact is: Every day care center, whether it knows it or not, is a school. The choice is never between custodial care and education. The choice is between unplanned and planned education, between conscious and unconscious education, between bad education and good education.

Most of the parents who today turn to day care centers are driven to them by sheer economic necessity. They must work or their family situation is so strained that they have no alternative. It is tragic when such already distressed families are forced to turn to centers which aim only at custodial care.

An increasing number of mothers today choose to work; they do not have to work for economic reasons. Many work for the sake of their child. They want more income for future education or for a nicer home or for more comforts. It is ironic as well as tragic when these parents find themselves forced to turn to custodial care centers. Most ease their consciences by blithely assuming: If no one is teaching, the child isn't learning. Many would be deeply dismayed to know some of the side-learnings that children are drinking in.

It is easy to leap to an unrealistic "solution": Make every mother stay at home! There is a better solution: Provide public day care centers. With adequate tax support day care centers can have trained staffs, good equipment, a sound curriculum. They need not have passive programs and can have active programs with the resources with which to buy good teaching.

"Play" Schools

Nursery schools traditionally have been scornful of custodial care. Many, however, have their own brand of passive program. Such nursery schools frequently have good play equipment; they may well have ample space; they usually give the youngsters great freedom. But once the teacher has set the stage she has done her good deed for the day. She turns the children loose, injecting herself only rarely to prevent accidents or when there is a bad quarrel. These nursery schools would not be found dead with a television set. Their big money is apt to go, as wastefully, into swings or a merry-go-round.

Their passivity stems in part from inadequate goals. Such schools think only of socialization. Their one big concern is to help children learn to live together, to get along together, to share and to cooperate. Their concept of good socialization is apt to be more wholesome than the confining and stereotyped aims of those kindergartens which focus on pre-first-grade socialization. But the isolated concentration on any *single* goal — social development in the nursery school, cognitive development in the kindergarten—underestimates children's capacity to learn, misjudges the realities of life, and always needlessly narrows a program.

Promoting sound social development is a worthy educational goal — it is *one* worthy educational goal. But good schools are schools for the development of the *whole child*. They seek to help children develop to their maximum their social powers *and* their intellectual powers, their emotional capacities, their physical powers.

Three- and four-year-olds have not been hurt as much in passive nursery schools as have those children caught in custodial care centers, but they have not learned as much as they comfortably, readily could. The children usually are active. They learn a little from their use of materials. They learn a little from their age-mates. But their learnings are apt to be haphazard and spotty, and little of the learning is individualized. Chances to count, measure, and compare slip by. Opportunities to enrich vocabulary are unnoticed. Opportunities to provoke thinking about cause and effect are ignored. Factual misunderstandings are not heard and not clarified. The teacher is on the sidelines. No adult is close in enough on what the children are doing to take advantage of the opportunities at hand.

Even in the top-prized area of social learnings, the teacher stays aloof except for crises. The materials and the equipment do all of the teaching; the adult looks on, usually from a distance. The children teach each other; the adult looks on, usually from a distance. Sound learnings about ways of living together may emerge, or individuals may as easily learn to give in, to go along with strength, to give up. The teacher is simply the safety supervisor, not the skilled yet unobtrusive leader who sensitively knows when to step in to reenforce sound learnings and to clarify and to avert miseducative happenings.

The passivity of these schools stems also from their overeagerness to let the child have fun. They escalate *play* from its rightful position as one of the prized methods of good education to an end in and of itself. These are "play-play-play" schools, not schools which wisely use play as one solid means of helping children to learn. They have one standard which to them justifies any activity, no matter what: "The children love it!"

This measuring rod — "The children love it!" — is a kindly standard, a gentle one. "Play-play-play" schools can take pride in their sensitive concern for feeling the tone of a child's daily life. Regrettably, there are schools which do not care enough whether or not a child is happy, whether or not he is pleased with what he is doing. This is most unfortunate. A school's job is to give children life, not to rob them of it. Early education must value highly each child's happiness; it must never lose a deep concern for bringing joy to children's days. But the educational challenge is to bring this joy through maximum learning.

"The children love it!" can justify an excursion (not a carefully planned field experience) to the ice cream plant — "They always give the youngsters a popsicle at the end." It can justify an overexciting, confusing, wearying voyage to the county fair or to the circus or to see a parade. It can justify taking no trips at all and never varying the equipment indoors or out-of-doors—the children seem to be playing happily enough.

Youngsters must love what they are doing. Their "love" — their
rapt attention, their voluntary self-selection — is the surest indica-
tor of their readiness and the best guarantee of retention of learning. But *what the children are doing* has to be an educator's first
concern. Young children are our newcomers. They are wide open.
The most amazing array of novelties will please them. They can
have fun watching a movie cartoon. They even take a bemused
sort of pleasure in a story they do not understand. Most can go
on day after day contentedly enough "just playing," living off their
home experiences, living off what they see on TV, getting no new
stimulus and challenge from their school. They can "love" (or like
or be willing enough, if nothing better is available) to go down a
slide they have gone down a thousand times before. But this is not
enough.

A good school is not a parking lot, a custodial care center.
Neither is it an amusement park, a "play-play-play" school.

Young children need ample chance to play. They need the
chance continuously at school throughout all the early childhood
years. But they need the chance to play in response to provocative
stimulation. They must be playing out — sorting out, trying out
— in response to a rich stream of mind and body and feeling-
stretching experiences flowing in to them. Good programs carefully,
consciously, confront children with the most significant experiences
available. Then consciously, sensitively, teachers help children
learn the most possible from these experiences. Youngsters love
this, too. A child has his deepest, truest "fun" when he functions
at his best.

Passivity in many nursery schools stems from inadequate goals.
It stems from confusion of method and goal. It stems from poor
implementation of method. But all these causes usually have their
root in that persistent devil — lack of money! School days have
lift and bounce when teachers plan the right experiences for their
youngsters and give children whatever help is needed. This
demands active, not passive teachers — teachers skilled in opening
up new choices, new challenges. It demands careful, continuous
planning, not the same old thing day after day. It requires a
personalized program, not turning children loose.

These fine teaching skills cost money. Like private colleges, no
nursery school can operate well on tuition-income alone. Few

parents are wealthy enough to pay all the costs of good education. Until there is tax support for public nursery schools, nursery education is in danger of becoming a part-time job for part-time people with partial training. Too many children who go to private nursery schools will continue to receive partial, passive early education.

TOP-QUALITY EDUCATION UNDER SIX

Many lucky youngsters get off to a good start. Despite the problems facing early education, there are outstanding nursery schools and day care centers, and have been for years. There are superb kindergartens. Many Head Start and Title I programs are excellent. The teachers in these good programs look to good theory as the basis for their curriculum. They deliberately build their programs on their best knowledge of why they are teaching, whom they are teaching, what they are teaching, and how they are teaching.

Teachers in these good programs keep their goals utterly clear. They aim to help their children learn, and to do it in such a way that the youngsters live their years of ages three and four and five in the richest, most satisfying, most constructive way possible. They keep their eyes consistently on the children in front of them.

Teachers in these good programs are child centered. They know what young children are like. Young children are different from older youngsters — they are not the same, simply cut down in size. These teachers' awareness of the special qualities of the very young colors everything that happens in their classroom. Their keen, sensitive understanding of child development is a prime factor in making these third and fourth and fifth years of life as pleasing and as productive for the children as they can possibly be.

Teachers in these good programs are society centered. They know and love our country, the best of its past and present. They hold bright hopes and conscious dreams for our future. These teachers' sense of democratic values colors everything that happens in their classroom. All of their relationships, everything they do, the whole life of the room is consistent with the finest qualities of our society: the values we hold dear and want to preserve, the values we want to nurture and help expand. These teachers know that young children are our future, but they know, too, that the future is not tomorrow — the future is now. The way young children live and learn today becomes the way they will live and learn tomorrow.

Teachers in these good programs are subject-matter centered. They know academic content and they know sound ways of teaching it to young children. Good classrooms for the very young teach the sciences and mathematics; they teach the social sciences; they teach the humanities; they teach health and physical education — as all schools of general education must. These good teachers are skilled in adapting these fields of learning to young children. Their methods are not unusual ones. Like teachers at all levels of education they, too, use lectures and discussions, tutoring and face-to-face instruction, laboratory and workshop sessions, buzz sessions and committee work, firsthand investigation, independent study, all kinds of audio-visual and other learning aids. But: they use these standard methods in the right proportion for the young children they teach. They use them wisely in ways that fit the age and fit our democratic society.

Teachers in these good programs have the tools they need to do their job. They have the right class size and the right ratio of adults to children. They have the space they need and the equipment. They have the professional freedom to do what they know should be done. Sometimes they have had to talk and argue and cajole and fight on behalf of their classrooms and their children but they know: If school is school is school, the same school for everyone regardless of age, it never is a good school for the very young. These teachers have what it takes — in spirit and in material stuff — to tailor-make their classrooms to fit the children who come.

2

A Child Centered Program

Young children are a special breed.

Children under six are different from the eight-year-olds and twelve-year-olds and sixteen-year-olds that our schools have served so long. They are so different that it is useful to think of early education as a kind of "special education."

Three- and four- and five-year-olds are exceptional children. They are not mentally retarded or physically handicapped or emotionally disturbed. They have their own kind of exceptionality that marks them off and demands special approaches: These children are *young*.

Some people think that Head Start children are the ones who are exceptional — poor children are the different ones. People who hold this opinion set Head Start youngsters apart from all other young children. They envisage a program for them that is different in nature from all other programs for the very young.

25

It is not accurate to draw a line between Head Start children and other young children. All young children — the children of the poor, the children of the rich — have a typical style and a typical swing in common. These qualities stem from the children's age and developmental status. They flow from the children's human nature. These qualities are not drastically changed by family income or geographic location or other external factors. They come with being young and all young children share them — Head Start youngsters, nursery and kindergarten and day care children.

Individual boys and girls, because of family background or personal traits, may show some of these special qualities to a more marked or lesser extent. Groups—Head Start youngsters, children of affluence — may exhibit some of them in a more accentuated or diminished fashion. Slight age-level differences show themselves as the children move from age three to four to five. The variations are minor, however. These are deep-rooted characteristics, pervasive characteristics, and they stamp all young children in the whole age range.

The right distinction is between *all* young children and all older youngsters. The line of distinction is commonly drawn at age six, but it should not be. Six-year-olds have a great deal in common with children under six. Sixes share all the qualities that go with being young that are described in the following pages; they are involved in the same basic growth tasks that children under six face. The real dividing line between early childhood and middle childhood is not between the fifth year and the sixth year — it is more nearly when children are about seven or eight, moving on toward nine. Building the barrier at age six has no psychological basis. It has come about only from the historic-economic-political fact that the age of six is when we provide schools for all.

In at least a dozen specific ways — other specialists might list more — young children flow differently from their older brothers and sisters. They have their own way of operating. Some of these qualities-of-being-young can be irritating for adults to live with. Some are difficult qualities for the usual school to take into account. But young children are made this way — this is their nature. The capacity and the willingness to live with these qualities make the crucial distinction between a good classroom for young children and one that does not fit the age.

THE STYLE AND SWING OF THE YOUNG

Young Children Are Not Good Sitters

Give them time and some day they will stay seated. Give them five or ten years. Then they will love to lounge and loaf, to stretch out, to stay put and take it easy. At this special point in their develpment three- and four- and five-year-olds are people on the go.

They can sit. They will sit — briefly at a table for juice; briefly sprawled on the floor for a story; briefly hunched on their chairs working on a puzzle. But sitting is not the young child's natural, comfortable position. It is not the pose he often chooses or stays in long.

Energy is popping inside these boys and girls. And the world around them always seems unusually alluring. These are active children, seldom still, seldom on a chair. They would make very bad office workers; they make a very bad audience. They feel almost all of the time what older children feel some of the time: "Don't tie me down . . . Don't fence me in."

Young children need room. They need two classrooms. They need ample space indoors for one; they need even more generous and private space outside for their very own outdoor classroom. The standard has been 35 square feet per child indoors, but this is minimal, really too little. Forty-five to 50 square feet of open, usable space per child is more nearly right. Out-of-doors the accepted standard of 200 square feet per child seems to be adequate. Providing this needed fenced outdoor classroom is a great challenge to urban schools with no playground — sites where many Head Start programs and day care centers are located. Roof tops may have to be converted to outdoor classroom use. Or, at the least, challenging "outdoor" equipment must be available at times indoors so that young children have the chance they are so eager for to perfect their body skills.

Indoors and out, young children need room for an eight-ring circus, not a mere three-ring one. The space is important because there must be something for children to do in everything that goes on. These boys and girls cannot simply sit, listen, watch, and still be true to their nature. A good classroom for them cannot operate on the premise that a child must sit down in order to learn. A good teacher has the know-how to teach active children significant learnings even though the youngsters are on the move much of the time. Any school that urgently needs to save money should not buy chairs or at least not one for every child. Chairs ought to be the least used equipment in early education.

Young Children Are Not Good at Keeping Quiet

Young children can, and do, keep quiet — for brief and exceptional periods of time. They are quiet when they are asleep. They are quiet some of the time when their mouths are full eating. They are quiet when someone talks to them personally, face-to-face. They are quiet through some but seldom all of a story.

Young children can be quiet but, at this point in life, silence is not golden. Young children enjoy noise for its own sake. The activity that means the most to them makes noise. Their moving about makes noise. They say what comes into their minds, and they want to talk with their friends.

Young children are subject, as we all are, to the fatigue of overstimulation and to the tension of confusion. Pandemonium will get them down. But the sounds of a laboratory or of a workshop, the happy sounds of friends, work sounds, do not bother them. Good order in a young child's classroom — good working conditions — differs from the order and quiet of a library or a church, and from that of the book-centered classroom.

Young children need freedom to talk as they play and work. They are the ones — not the teacher — who do most of the talking in a good classroom. The size of their groups must be right so that the natural noise of busy people does not mount simply because there are too many people. Their rooms must be situated — or acoustically treated, or people in nearby classrooms must understand — that hammering and laughter, drums and a piano, blocks falling and children's conversation do not become crises for a whole school. A good classroom for young children need not be so quiet that you can hear a pin drop before a child can learn.

Young Children Are Shy

Children under six are not yet "hale fellows well met." They love people and are fascinated by them, but they love people best in small doses. Masses overwhelm the young child.

Young children are at their best in a class of 10, 12, 15, 20 children — depending on their age. This is not small class size, for them. For them this is *full* class size, up to the brim and almost overflowing. These children are just beginning, gingerly and tentatively, to thread their way into the wider world. These are shrinking violets, so easily stamped back by crowds into an uncomfortable sense of their own littleness.

Even right class size has to be broken down into still smaller subgroups, into safe personal clusters. Then the young child really blossoms out. Face-to-face with his teacher he can be at ease. Face-to-face with another child — or with two or three or four other children — he can be talkative and a good listener, comfortable and responsive. If he has to spend much of his time in the group as a whole, even a class of right size can seem to him like Grand Central Station or Times Square on New Year's Eve. The young child needs a teacher who is not under a compulsion to keep the whole group together around her. His teacher has to be mobile and move around as much as the child does.

A child needs a room with nooks where he can be by himself at times, alone with a book or puzzle or game. He needs a room that is large enough so that, most of the time, he can work with two or three or four other children. The child under six is not yet a "joiner," not yet ready to shout "Hail, hail, the gang's all here." He gets along beautifully if you let him make his own definition of "gang": a small, intimate, little group.

Young Children Are Highly Egocentric

At some far future point, if their growth has been healthy, these children will be able to think in terms of a team, a mate, a family, a nation, a world. Now they are in the very early springtime of this life-long development. They are aware of *themselves*. Their one clear point of reference is an intensely personal one.

Their keenest interest lies in themselves. This self-centeredness shows in their greeting: "I have new shoes" . . . "I have a new belt." Their truly precious self is in every train of thought and pops out in interruptions of story and discussion and conversation: "I have a puppy" . . . "I went to the hospital once." All their understanding ties back to themselves: "My daddy shaves" . . . "My mommy works" . . . "My uncle is visiting us" . . . "I saw a policeman." On every issue the vote is the same: The "I's" have it!

Not so long ago these children were not even aware that they existed as separate individuals, persons apart. Now they are overwhelmed by this awareness and expect the whole world to be equally amazed. "Old hands" — more certain of who they are and what they are like, more accepting of their limitations, clearer on their powers — can relax. These "new hands" are full of themselves. They want to make choices. They have to have preferences. They love to take the initiative, to have an idea and carry it out themselves. Eventually these children will come, if their life goes right, to follow the commandment: *Love thy neighbor as thyself.* Right now they are taking the first step: Children under six are learning to love themselves.

Their teacher must have the time to listen to each one, the time to praise and, most important, the willingness to puff up each child. Our adult attitude is so important. Good teachers believe that, given healthy growth, a strong social sense will develop in good time. But now is the time for a sense of personal worth. It is all too easy, in the name of morality, to suppress this budding individuality. We have to be glad to see each child blossom.

In one way the young child's egocentricity ought to make all of us glad: It gives us a good grasp on curriculum. So long as the child sees himself in the picture, you can be sure his interest and enthusiasm will be high.

Young Children Want to Feel Proud, Big, and Important

Success matters very much to the under-six age group. These children want so desperately to be able to hold their heads high.

They sound exceedingly boastful: "I can count up to five" . . . "I can tie my shoes" . . . "I know how old I am. Do you want to see?" . . . "I fell and I didn't even cry." Each child maintains his own public relations office. He is continuously concerned with getting his name and his skill and his knowledge and his power into the "headlines." But we mustn't be misled by this drum-beating. The bombast is as much for the child's benefit as for ours — he can't quite believe his own importance.

For all their braggadocio, these are still very incompetent children. A hundred times a day their smallness, their ignorance, their limited capacities bring them face to face with an irritating, frustrating fact: They are still little shavers, they still cannot do very much. Inescapably they confront things they can't reach, things they can't lift, things they can't carry, things they can't see but want to see.

Success tastes so sweet because it comes all too seldom. No wonder young children beat the drums whenever there is cause for celebration: "I can write my name. Do you want to see me?" . . . "I can hop on one foot. Watch!" . . . "I can climb all the way up to the top!" The rumble of the drums makes achievement seem like an every-minute event. The child wishes it were; in reality success is rare.

Added man-made failure really hurts young children. No one has to contrive lessons for these youngsters so that they will learn how to lose — they are losers too much of the time. No one has to put them in their place — they know all too well in their hearts the little place they are in. No one has to cut them down to size — their size is painfully small. At this stage in their development we are wise to stay away from competition, from games and races and contests with winners and losers. It matters too much to each child to come in first — they cannot stand the risk of competition.

A good classroom offers many ways in which many children can know glory. It must not have a program which prizes only certain kinds of abilities, a track where the race is only to the swift. It must have many jobs that youngsters can do, many responsibilities they can carry, the widest variety of burdens and challenges — mountains to climb — within the capacity of the widest variety of children. Each day each child must go home with his head held higher — that is each child's heart's desire.

Young Children Have Their Private Dream World

Boys and girls under six perform many realistic, honest-to-goodness jobs. They learn many down-to-earth facts and build many practical skills. It is up to us to plan the environment so that they know objective success often during a day. But young children also have an insurance policy: They live a large part of their time in a private dream world, one they themselves plan and manage and control beautifully. In their dream world things always work out as they should. In this inner world each child can be as strong and powerful and masterful as ego demands. Each child is guaranteed all the sympathy, support, love, and tenderness that any loser could ask.

This dream world is the child's private world of play and pretend. He creates it through his own imagination. Make-believe serves many developmental purposes. It is the arena for much of the young child's early thinking, planning, organizing. Intellectual processes go on in play that are foundational to all the clear reasoning that the child will be capable of later. Make-believe is the avenue to much of the young child's early understanding. He sorts out impressions and tries out ideas that are foundational to his later realistic comprehension. This private world sometimes is a quiet, solitary world. More often it is a noisy, busy crowded place where language grows, and social skills develop, and where perseverance and attention-span expand. But always underneath, while all these other purposes are being served, play and pretend is also the young child's private protected port.

Older, more confident people have less need of dream worlds. Only at rare times do they turn to their inner imaginary conversations, their brief flights of daydreaming, their Walter Mitty moments. Young children, so unsure and so open to hurt, have a continuous need for settings where they can make the rules — "This must be our garage and this must be our car"; and where they can control the outcomes — "This must be my birthday and you must bring me a present"; and where they are the masters — "I must be the doctor and you must be sick."

At the under-six age, reality — accuracy, the facts, what actually goes on, how things really work — must not dominate the day. Teachers must be skilled in knowing how to encourage rich fantasy, how to stimulate a child's own free and spontaneous make-believe world. Play is so important developmentally that going to school must not rob the child of his chance to pretend.

Young Children Are Very Tender

Young children need to know that they are loved. Every human, even the strongest among us, shares this hunger. But young children are dependent in the extreme. They are the newcomers to our earth. The aliens. The strangers. They are feeling their way, just getting the hang of things. So much is strange, incomprehensible. They must be able to turn with full faith to the old-timers, the people who know their way around.

Older children have more resources within themselves. The young child's pillars of support are his parents and his teachers. When these supports seem angry or cold or aloof or disinterested or busy, the young child has nothing. He is left alone and that is more than he can bear. The young child wants to grow in his own strength, but he has to grow from a position of safety. He needs big people in whom he can put his trust.

These are affectionate youngsters. They are demonstrative at times. Wordy assurances of love do not always fill the bill. Young children come to us for a kiss or a squeeze. Many times they look to us for the physical proof that all is well. They seek sympathy, the playful pat, the gentle arm, the friendly hand. Their classroom cannot be an impersonal, standoffish place.

Most of all, it cannot be a harsh, angry, dissatisfied classroom because they need so deeply to count on our goodwill. Young children scare easily — a tough tone, a sharp reprimand, an exasperated glance, a peeved scowl will do it. Little signs of rejection — you don't have to hit young children to hurt them — cut very deeply. Sometimes their response fools us. In their panic when they feel they are not loved, young children often act worse. If they are to be at their very best, their classroom must be suffused with gentleness and warmth.

Young Children Are Beginners

Their classroom must be suffused with patience and tolerance, too. Young children are life's amateurs. They make all kinds of mistakes, as any fumbling beginner must. Give the young child a kitten and he squeezes it too hard. Let him touch a baby and he touches too roughly. He spills his juice. He knocks over the blocks. He runs where people should walk. He makes noise in many situations where older people are quiet. When he first tries to write his name he writes it backwards. He punches and pinches and grabs at times, even though when you talk to him he "knows" he should not. The young child is a mistake-prone child.

He makes his errors in part because his coordination is still so uncertain. He errs in part because his emotions are so strong. Because he is so inexperienced, so uninformed. Because so many of life's big lessons simply take a long time to learn. He "knows" a little about these lessons but he hasn't mastered them — and he forgets.

The patience we all need in living with the young child comes more easily if we remember: *He has time!* He has years stretching out ahead of him. The chances are great indeed that today's young child will finish high school. Start him in school at the age of three and he has fifteen years of formal schooling ahead. The

chances increase all the while that today's young child will go on
to some form of college — he probably has seventeen or nineteen
years of formal schooling ahead. By the time of his young adult-
hood, graduate or specialized or technical training will be even
more common than it is today. He may well have twenty or twenty-
one years of schooling ahead of him. More and more of today's
youngsters will live to the age of ninety — they will live in a time
when there will be better and easier means of informal schooling
and of independent study. The child in nursery school today may
well have eighty-seven years for learning stretching out ahead.

Time is not running out for young children. Time is just
beginning.

The young child's classroom, more than any other grade level,
ought to be free of cram sessions. More than any other, it should
be tension-free. It ought to be calamity-free and crisis-free. Mistakes must be corrected and the right ways must be learned, but
no one in a panic ought to feel that he has to stuff these beginners
quickly with social or physical or emotional or intellectual learnings.

Young children have the time *and* they need the time. Intellectually they cannot incorporate learnings into themselves with
words said once, words said quickly. They need more than a
once-over-lightly approach. Emotionally they cannot stand the
pace of acceleration and pressure. Their classroom has to run
on slow time; it shouldn't have a stop watch with a split-second
hand. After all, these are the children who at home and at school
beg to hear the same story over and over again. The adult, not
the child, is in a hurry to move on, thinking "Oh, no! Not that
same one again!"

Young Children Are Hungry for Stimulation

Their pace is slow. They repeat themselves. They are not readily
bored by what can seem to quick-moving, quick-thinking, knowledgeable adults like "the same old thing." But young children are
not *blasé*. They want to learn. They are curious. They carry within
them — they have since they were born — a sharp hunger for
stimulation.

When they were crib-bound babies, their minds were not idle.
As infants these children busily used their eyes as their first
investigators—roaming, peering, probing. Their fingers have been
tools for learning ever since they could make their hands and eyes
work together. Just as soon as those exploring hands could carry

objects to the mouth they have used their lips and tongue to find out about the world. They have tasted and sucked more weird things than parents care to remember. Once language developed, children began and have persisted with a steady, wearying stream of questions. These are slow learners — they like to take their time. But these are not reluctant scholars. They are the most eager age ever to walk into a school.

In school they continue to want to see, to touch and handle and use, to taste, and to sniff. Words alone seldom satisfy the deep-rooted curiosity of this age. Call young children cynics. Call them skeptics. Say they all come from Missouri. They prefer not to take anyone's word or to take much on faith. They want to test things out for themselves.

It was this drive for stimulation, this hunger to find out, that alerted middle-class, conscientious parents that their child needed more than their home alone could provide: "I can't keep up with him" . . . "He's always getting into things." Now that the child is in nursery school or kindergarten (or day care or Head Start), the group must not coop him up or tone him down or dull and deaden this curiosity. Because he is in a group it has to be easier, not harder, to confront him with objects, people, events for all those good tools — eyes, ears, nose, mouth, fingers — to explore.

The young child's two classrooms — indoors and outdoors — must be rich in variety, rich in newness, rich in challenge. They must be open classrooms: open-shelved, with youngsters free to explore the feast before their eyes, and open-doored, with youngsters freer to explore the world outside their schoolroom because they are in school. "Going to" school need not mean "staying in" school. To satisfy this eager age school cannot mean a period of confinement and containment but the chance for wider exploration.

Young Children Are Earthy, Practical, Concrete-minded

Young children learn from words, of course. They have been talked with and at in their homes. In all schools — inevitably, necessarily—they will still be talked with and at. But words alone— symbols, substitutes for the real thing — are not yet their best means of learning. Words, in fact, can fool them: They think they understand. Words can fool us, too: *We* think they understand.

Today's child often is a good talker. He gives the impression of being very smart, but some of his smartness is simply his "line." The TV he has seen, the talk he has heard, give him a veneer.

He can become a good parakeet, but *understanding* is the young child's goal. It ought to be our goal, too.

Young children are starting from scratch. It sounds harsh to say "They are ignorant," but they do know so very little. They have to pile up the specifics, pile up the incidents, pile up the situations so that they can have a solid base of things they do understand. Then they have something concrete to which they can tie down new ideas as they come along. Then they can use symbols with a clearer, truer sense of knowing what they stand for.

A good classroom for young children is not in a hurry to skip over the real, the actual. It has to be glad to begin at the beginning. People always say: Experience is the best teacher. It certainly is the foundational teacher. And, because of that, it is the ideal teacher for the very young. These youngsters can make the greatest sense out of what they have had the chance, at firsthand, to see and do and explore.

Young Children Are Acquiescent

Young children — new to the world, new to school — are not yet in a position to be critics. They have to take things as they come. They have to assume that whatever happens is the natural order of events. This acquiescence is part of the young child's armor against trauma and tragedy. It is part of his protection against the many disasters that say to older people: "Something is wrong!" Young children make only the simple assumption: "This is life — you go along."

This naïvité is compounded by the young child's dependence on adult goodwill. He stands ready to go along with whatever adults seem to want. He stands poised, trying to figure out what they want. The young child is almost at the mercy of adults — it is so important to him to please. This is a hazardous position for a child whose developmental need is to be pleased with himself.

This combination of newness and dependence means: It is easy to take advantage of young children. With only a little force, with only a little sweetness, teachers can make young children jump through hoops for them. Teachers in good classrooms have to bend over backwards not to manipulate youngsters. Teachers must be strong adults who are not afraid to be adults when a child needs the strength that only an adult can have. But these strong adults must also be humble adults — uncommonly honest with themselves. They must constantly ask themselves about the activities in their room: "Whose idea was it?" "Whom does it please?"

Older children are more apt to fight back when they are exploited or pushed around. Young children do too occasionally — they are not good all the time. They have their moments of rebellion, but they are more apt to try hard to play the game, whatever the game may be.

The teacher looks and sees willing faces. She must be uncommonly honest in assessment. Do these signify mere lukewarm going-along? Or children's wholehearted, full-bodied desire? Young children's easy acquiescence can make it difficult to tell.

A wise classroom teacher offers many choices. She counts a lot on self-selection, on children freely "voting" for what they will do and with whom they will do it and how long they will continue to do it. The "votes" are not by written or spoken ballot but by behavior. In a climate of freedom, in a setting of many worthwhile possibilities, what children choose to do is apt to stem from deeper, more significant strands than simple acquiescence. Children's self-selection is the teacher's best insurance policy against inadvertently imposing and intruding and over-controlling.

Young Children Are Illiterate

A few children begin to learn to read as young as age three. A few more begin around four. A larger handful begin when they are five. Yet even the most advanced, most precocious of these early readers are still in the dog-paddling stage. They are a far cry from being able to get from the printed page the rich flood of stimulation all children need.

And these early readers are the exception. The overwhelmingly largest number of children under six are not yet even dog-paddling. They are not yet hanging on to the side of the pool practicing their kick. They are not yet even in the water. Even those who can read a little — certainly all the rest who cannot and who could not care less — are illiterate. This is an obvious characteristic of young children, and sometimes the most infuriating of all.

People worry so much about reading at an early age today, and some of this worry is quite needless. The chance to read surrounds young children: words on the TV screen, labels and signs in every store and on every product, billboards and street markers and highway signs, the words in books, newspapers, comics, letters, notes, calendars . . . . Reading is a skill that brings young children one area of delicacy in their life: mastery, power, control. Once a child has this mastery he becomes an extra-lucky child. The world of the far-away is opened to him. The world of the gone-by is opened to him. He is no longer tied to the small world of his own experience. Such an attractive, appealing "product," available everywhere a child turns, requires no hard sell. There is no need, anxiously and nervously, to push it.

Nor is there any argument at all against helping young children move toward this fabulous power, helping each one of them move as fast as he can comfortably go. Youngsters themselves will want to leave their illiteracy behind them, just as they want to leave their dependency behind and just as they want to leave their ignorance behind. But each child must set his own pace. The urge to read blossoms in different children at different times. The strong argument that can be made is against forcing all children to begin at the same time. This hurts too many youngsters, and it spoils reading for too many.

There is a strong argument, too, against saying: "Reading is the *only* way of getting smart at an early age — you have to learn to read first and then we can teach you other things." A good classroom can be geared to illiterates. It capitalizes on what children *can* do: They can see, they can hear, they can ask, they can touch, they can talk . . . . It makes the most of the powers they do have to teach them no end of worthwhile learnings, before children learn to read *and* as they learn to read. This is the kind of classroom young children need.

Individual Differences

Young children have one other special quality which must be mentioned. This characteristic is not "special" because it marks young children off from older boys and girls. It is extra-special because it is so important: There are great individual differences among young children. Provision for diversity is an imperative in good early education, just as it is in all good education.

There Are Great Individual Differences Among Young Children

In the under-six years children are in the process of taking many giant developmental strides. These are years of transition and of great movement in many fundamental growth areas. Young children are moving from dependence toward independence. From clumsy coordination to finer skills. From body talk to verbal communication. From a strong reliance on outer control to a developing inner control. From imagination toward reality. From exclusive personal awareness to growing social concern. From the here-and-now to wider intellectual awareness. From illiteracy to a deepening interest in symbols.

The young children who make up a classroom can be at many different places along these various paths of growth. And individual children can be at different places on different days. The overall growth process is steady but unstable — children can spurt ahead, they can slide back, they can seemingly stay still for periods. A good classroom seeks to know exactly where each child stands on these many paths and to be geared to him where he is.

It is so easy to lump children. We tend to put them in a pile, put a label on the pile, and think we never again have to look at the people in the pile.

Head Start boys and girls, in particular, face this danger. They face it twice-over today. Some teachers mistakenly assume that these children are different from all other children. Then they mistakenly assume that everyone is alike within the Head Start pile. We label the youngsters: "culturally disadvantaged" . . . "economically underprivileged" . . . "children of the poor." Once we put the label on we find it harder to see: *These are all individuals.* Each has his own history. Each his own personal family. Each has his own inborn capacities and his own rate of growing. The label can blind us. We see the tag but we cannot see the child.

Some youngsters in Head Start have an unusually deep need for affection. Poverty living has robbed them of adults who might have had the time and the spirit to give the tender care that all young children need. These youngsters are starved for love. *Some* children in Head Start are. Many may be. But not all. Other youngsters who live in poverty come from warm and deeply loving homes. They have a strong inner sense of security, much sturdier than that of some economically advantaged children. Homes of the wealthy can be houses full of things, but empty of people who take the time to show their love.

Some Head Start children may seem wild. They may act as if they have never known discipline. Poverty can take adults out of the home, leaving the children free to roam. But some children who have grown up in poverty have experienced very severe, overly strict, almost repressive discipline. And some, of course, have had the reasonable limits that young children thrive on.

Some boys and girls who have grown up in poverty have more language handicaps than other young children do. Some of them, that is; not necessarily all. Some may be more distractable. Some may be less interested in books. Some may be more independent. Some may have great body skills. Some may seem less curious and some may already be persuaded that they cannot succeed. The key word is *some!* Labels can usefully alert us to the probabilities, but we must not confuse probability with certainty. Our eyes have to stay on each child, not his tag.

Unless we specifically guard against it, the Head Start label can make us think: "All these children are stupid — if you are poor you must be stupid." Scores on initial tests, given by strange people in strange settings in a strange form of their language, can firm up the stereotype. Once we build a fixed opinion there is the danger that children will, in fact, live down to it. We have to remind ourselves constantly: There are some retarded children in Head Start groups; there are many more of good average ability; there are some who have superior innate power. The label must not make us prejudge.

But Head Start children are not the only ones with labels. We put other children in piles, too: "immature" children, only children, high IQ children . . . . We even build generalities about boys and girls — their sex becomes a label. Putting children in categories so we can talk about them is hard to stop, but to teach children well we have to zero in. The essence of knowing children is knowing each child well.

Tailoring a Program to Fit

A good teacher has a series of sharp, individual portrait photographs etched in her mind. She is leery of group pictures. Then this personal information must be put to work. Knowing individuals is not an academic exercise; it provides the data for tailoring a program to fit each and every child.

Teachers of young children must use every approach to bring each youngster to life as a distinct person. Visiting youngsters at home, seeing each in his own familiar setting, has to become standard operating procedure. Class size and teacher load must make such visits easily possible. There must be time for personal walks and talks alone with individual children. Finding time to observe each child carefully at school — how he stands and how he talks, what he does and with whom he does it, his speed and style — has to become a built-in part of each teaching day. Youngsters cannot always be seen *en masse*.

A teacher needs to learn as much about a child's earlier development as parents, the child's doctor, and any previous teachers can report. A teacher needs to know as much about his present status as every kind of test — physical examinations, mental tests, achievement tests, emotional and social inventories — can reveal. She needs to know a child's whole day and whole week and whole month and year — not only the hours of the school day but the full day and weekends, too.

There ought to be no impersonal, one-way report cards in under-six education. Parents and teachers need to talk together. They need to talk before school opens and often once school is under way. Conferences ought to be the established form of reporting. There should be no hesitancy about closing school for children, if need be, so parents can come to school. Communication between parents and teachers is an essential, not a luxury, in under-six education.

A good classroom cannot be tailored to fit "almost all" the youngsters — it must be right for everyone. A good test of this custom-approach is our attitude at the start of school. "Almost all" young children will feel at home in school in a short time, especially if the start is gentle and patient. Young children should never come trooping in all at once on opening day, strangers to each other, strangers to the teacher. Nursery schools, kindergartens, Head Start need many "opening days." Children ought to come in small groups so they won't feel lost in the crowd. The hours at the start ought to be shorter than usual so that the separation from home is gradual. Mothers should be encouraged to stay, when their child needs them or when they need their child. Treated sensitively, warmly, "almost all" young children will take this crucial separation in their stride.

But there is no reason why a Billy who needs his mother for two or three weeks or for a month cannot have her in school with him, if she is free to stay. There is no reason why a Grace who loves school for two hours and then worries during the last half-hour cannot go home early, if transportation is no problem. There is no reason why a favorite blanket or doll cannot come to school with the child who needs it to help him feel safe.

There are countless other "tests" of our commitment to individual differences, once the program is fully underway. A good kindergarten — a good nursery school or day care program or Head Start — must be geared for the Sue who is entranced with reading, as well as for all the others who show minimal signs of interest. Sue has to be able to hear tens of stories, while the others may be content with one at "official" story time. Sue has to be able to dictate her own stories, one after the other, as many as her strong drive demands. Her dramatic play must be embellished with signs and labels and all kinds of appropriate writing — this won't hurt the others playing with Sue but it will make her life more meaningful. She must be able to play countless matching games, pairing objects or letters or words as her reading ability dictates. There must be a typewriter in Sue's classroom for her to turn to whenever she wishes, and printing sets. She must have books without stint to read on her own: primers and easy-to-read trade books, books of her own-dictated stories, whatever her taste and ability. And she must, of course, have all the teacher-help she needs as she reads, whenever she needs it. Class size and staffing must make this personalized approach possible. No Sue should ever have to slow down because she is in a group, nor should anyone else have to speed up because Sue is in the group.

Some of today's children know a great deal more than young children of the past. Their parents have spent hours with them, answering their questions, reading stories to them, and taking them on trips. For many of them the family automobile has been a "school," taking them places that yesterday's children never saw. These youngsters have been in on family conversations, not shut out and set apart. They have heard adult ideas and events discussed. Almost all of them have been exposed to a variety of television programming.

The child with a solid store of information must not be bored in nursery school or kindergarten or day care. He needs the chance to pursue activities in depth so that they become as challenging to him as they are to the child who has a more meagre background. A daily program is not an election which the majority wins. Majority and minority have equal rights. No one can be shortchanged.

Rules must be adjusted to the child who needs clear limits, to the child who needs elbowroom, and to the many who need only a few reasonable regulations. We must make every effort to adjust schedules to the child enamored of climbing, to the one bitten by the tricycle bug, to the child who could paint until the cows come home. Stronger interest, greater gift, special need, slower speed must not set the pace for all. Neither must these personal qualities be lost in the shuffle as the price a child pays for being in a group.

WHO GETS READY? CHILD OR SCHOOL?

Can we have good schools for young children with this baker's dozen of special qualities?

Some communities say: "No . . . . The children are too young . . . They are 'immature'." These schools keep raising their entrance age — a child must be 5.9 or 5.10 or 5.11 by the start of school.

The fact is, however: Most three-year-olds, almost all four-year-olds, the very largest number of five-year-olds, are mature enough, developmentally ready, to go . . . somewhere. These are young children but they feel independent. They want to venture out. They have reached a point where they need to be with people their own age. They want to go places and do things.

Young children do not usually end up in a group because their mothers have pushed them out. The children are reaching out. They are propelled by the same hunger for stimulation that sends the freshman eagerly off to college. The drive for companionship, for challenge, does not begin at age six or eighteen. It shows clearly in most children around age three. By then, certainly at age four, almost always at age five the young child is ready for school . . . if the school can be ready for him.

Raising the school entrance age is a backward approach. It has been well demonstrated that there is no great trick in running a good school even for two-year-olds. Exclusion policies are only appropriate if a school conceives of its first grade as a fixed package — you have to buy it "as is." The child must be ready, the school cannot get ready. But this is such a stubborn, unnecessary rigidity.

Life and Ways of the Two Year Old *by Louise Woodock (New York: E.P. Dutton & Co., Inc., 1941; New York: Basic Books, Inc., Publishers, 1952) discusses early education programs for this age group.*

Still other schools know all the characteristics of young children and say: "Ah ha! Come!" "Young children are active . . . noisy . . . shy . . . egocentric . . . boastful . . . illiterate . . . ." These schools will change all that. They are dying to get their hands at least on some of the youngsters. They don't want three- or four-year-olds — they are too young. They don't want anything to do with day care — that is not their business. But five-year-olds! Especially poverty children whose homes and communities have not taught them all they should know! These schools can hardly wait.

Such schools do not feel "anti-child." They are persuaded that what they do is for the child's own good. Their rationale is: Youngsters have only this summer or this year, this brief time, in which to make up the gaps necessary to survive first grade. Once they get ready to read and learn the ropes, then they will have it made. The children will be honestly proud . . . They can be legitimately boastful . . . Their egos will be stronger . . . Success will breed success.

The doctrine is dangerous.

The qualities that come with being young are not imperfections or flaws. They are not minor irritants to be brushed aside lightly. Early childhood is a marked and definable stage in development with basic growth tasks that must be achieved at this time. We are naïve if we assume that we can ignore what children are like, plunge ahead manipulating and managing and forcing, and still get off scot free.

No one knows for sure what the price is of stopping young children's play, of curbing their initiative and spontaneity, of deadening their energy, of blocking their social exploration. But unless we want to assume that young children's style and swing are God's mistake, we must recognize: We are playing with fire when we skip the years of three, four, and five to hurry children into being age six.

The doctrine is immoral and unethical, too.

Every child has a right to his fifth year of life, his fourth year, his third year. He has a right to live each year with joy and self-fulfillment. No one should ever claim the power to make a child mortgage his today for the sake of tomorrow. The individual can choose to do this with his own life. He often does, in pursuing technical education or professional education or specialized education. But in general education — liberal education, humane education — the moral imperative stands clear: Today counts. Today becomes tomorrow but today is here. And important. And worthy.

Come As You Are

First grade need not be a black cloud that darkens all the days that precede it.

Nor must children's essential nature be exploited in order to make intellectual gains, social gains, emotional gains, physical gains.

We need say only one thing to young children: *Come as you are!* Come with your age-level characteristics. Come with those qualities that make you a unique and special person. Schools can have the flexibility and imagination and sensitivity to be ready for the children who come.

There is nothing daring about this. Schools now do this for many age levels. School is no one thing. It need not be one set thing. True: If you say "School," images come to everyone's mind. They are apt to picture desks, books, chalkboard, teacher up front talking, children sitting, children quiet, reading, writing, raising their hands.... But these are partial pictures. Some parts of some schools are like this. But in truth, schools are many things. They can have — they do have — the equipment, the supplies, the space, the class size, the administrative arrangements to fit the people who come to them.

Schools are playing fields and gymnasiums and stadiums. Schools are classes of one and classes of five; classes of ten and classes of several hundred. Schools are farms and camps and planes and stoves and refrigerators. They are test tubes, Bunsen burners, laboratory benches. Schools are lathes and print shops, lumber yards and metal shops. Schools have indoor classrooms; schools also have cow barns, hothouses, geologic diggings. Schools are typewriters, adding machines, computers, automobiles. Schools are studios. Not everyone who comes to school comes to sit, read, listen, be quiet.

Children come with their special needs: mental retardation, cardiac conditions .... They come with their special interests: home economics, agriculture, business education .... They come with their peculiar age-level demands: sports, dramatics, graduate seminars .... Good schools for older age levels are tailor-made to fit the students who come. Schools can be tailor-made to fit young children too.

It is time for communities and for school people to take pride in having the special adaptations that make school distinctively right, uniquely geared, beautifully fit for the three-, four- and five-year-olds who come.

Threes, fours, and fives deserve a child-centered program, not a first-grade-centered one. They need a program planned for their age, not a "pre" school which is a lackey of "regular" school. Threes, fours, and fives — nursery school, kindergarten, day care, Head Start — deserve a school that welcomes them for their own sake: *Come as you are!*

The DEW Line

In one legitimate way under-six education can be "the lackey" of over-six education. Rightly, without distortion to its own program, under-six education can be the public schools' DEW Line, the Distant Early Warning System. It can — consciously, deliberately — be the screening device to spot children early who have special problems so these youngsters can begin early to get the help they need.

Early education has a unique opportunity to serve this purpose. So good a chance will not come again. Because of the young child's dependency, the teacher has a golden opportunity to know parents. Because of the nature of a good program, the teacher has a golden opportunity to know children. Because of the age of the youngsters, the teacher has a golden opportunity to get beneath the surface. Young children are in motion more than older youngsters. They have not yet learned the disguises, how to cover up and hide their real selves. They are not yet quite civilized. When they are angry, they show it. When they are frightened, they show it. When they are worried, they show it. When they are pleased, they show it. The teacher of young children can get data easily that soon becomes hidden from other teachers.

One of the great gaps in public health is that children are not seen regularly by trained and objective eyes when they are young. Large numbers of children of the poor never see a physician after they are born. More fortunate youngsters receive good medical care prenatally, at the time of birth, and for the few months immediately following. Then, for the long span of years from early infancy until school entrance at age six, even these youngsters are viewed only through their parents' subjective and untrained eyes. The doctor is called in emergencies. Too often then he sees only the sickness and not the child. In these long years of gap physical and psychological problems can develop, grow in size, and become harder to correct the longer they stay unnoticed.

While some conscientious parents worry needlessly about their children, far too many do not worry enough. They live in hope. They are fully ready to believe that a child's slowness in talking or his great distractability or his tempestuous temper or his bad coordination are characteristic of all children. Their wish is father to the thought: "He'll outgrow it." Children do outgrow their normal, healthy, age-level characteristics. They do not outgrow their problems; these only become worse with the passing of time.

Our whole society pays a staggering price when we do not identify early and help early people who are in trouble. We know the price tag for police protection, for jails, for mental hospitals. We have no way of getting at the cost in wasted talent and wasted energy of people well enough to stay out of institutions but not well enough to function at their best. Millions needlessly sell themselves short. They carry prejudice and suspicion inside of themselves. They are angrier at life than they need be, more fighty than they need be, more compelled to be "anti" than they need be.

The American Academy of Pediatrics recognized the importance of early objective intervention years ago when it gave its blessing to the fledgling nursery school movement. The Academy saw the nursery school as a device necessitating a complete physical examination. It wanted some means to bring the seemingly well child back in touch with his doctor to be sure he was really well. Early intervention is more needed today and on an expanded scale: reaching all of our young children and with a wider concept of health, including mental as well as physical health, a concern for how the child feels about himself and people, how he relates to life around him. Early education can and should do this job.

Careful, complete physical examinations ought to be a "must" for all programs of early education, *plus* the start of any remedial treatment the examinations show the need for.

Careful, complete observational records by teachers ought to be a "must" for all programs of early education. These records should be passed on religiously to the next teacher. They should flow from the private nursery school or day care center to the kindergarten, without fail. They should go from Head Start to the kindergarten, from the kindergarten to first grade as a matter of firm, fixed policy. Sometimes, the next teacher does not want to see the records — she "wants to make up her own mind." It is up to her to be as much an isolationist as she has to be or as wise as she can be. But early education's responsibility is clear: We must pass on every understanding we have about our children.

Good teachers of young children strive hard for good discipline. With some badly hurt youngsters, however, success cannot be measured by whether or not a teacher can quickly make them act well. The task is to help them feel and be well, and this may take many years. The total school will have to work with these children for a long period of time. With such hurt youngsters the right measure of success is not: Did you make them toe the mark? The right measure is whether or not the under-six teacher began to understand them and whether or not she passed on her understandings to the teacher who follows. To help children with severe unmet needs we have to work as a team, one year building on the progress of the year before.

The insights passed on, of course, need not be confined to warnings of possible trouble. The largest number will relate to healthy youngsters and to good ways of working with them: Joe has a keen interest in motors ... Frankie is a delightfully verbal child with an extensive vocabulary .... Beth has beautiful coordination .... Tim is a highly social boy with truly winning ways .... Youngsters have many gifts that stay hidden unless there is a setting where the gifts can reveal themselves.

So soon the stage narrows down. The children sit, the children read. Only gifts of one particular kind — academic brilliance — get the spotlight. Children have — the world needs — a wide array of talent. We must not lose sight of the gift of humor, of imagination and creativity, of doggedness and perseverance; the gift of strength, of organizational ability, of sympathy, of bravery and courage .... As easily and as legitimately as it can be the warning system that sends out early alerts, under-six education can be the talent show that uncovers many stars for all the education that follows.

3

A Society Centered Program

Young children are a special breed. So, too, are Americans.

A school for young Americans ought to have a distinctively democratic flavor. It ought to have a way of going about things that marks it off from a school for young Chinese or Russian or Spanish children. American youngsters, living their third and fourth and fifth years of life, ought to breathe in the air of America. They ought to know our life, the best of what our country is now, the best that our country can be.

YOUNG AMERICANS

Schools are not only for the individual's benefit. Schools are for the benefit of us all. They are society's protection. They are our national insurance policy, the preserver of our common good, so that — educated — we don't slide back, so that — educated — we keep moving ahead.

It is easy to forget: Man is made and constantly being remade. Society is constantly being remade, too. Nothing — not peace nor

51

pain, not prosperity nor poverty, not pride nor prejudice — is guaranteed to last. Nothing inevitably persists, neither the desirable nor the hateful. No country, not even powerful America, ever "has it made," its bright future assured.

Change is evidenced throughout world history. We know of the fall of the Roman Empire, the ending of the power of the Greek city states, the waning of the once-great dominance of Egypt, China, Babylon, Turkey, the Incas . . . Variety of cultures is evidenced through anthropology. We have read of cultures where women dominate, where cannibalism is approved, where goods are owned communally. We have read of societies where to die is glorious, where this life matters not at all except as a painful brief passage.

Man is an assorted being. He is a various being. He has the potential to believe and to behave in the most amazing ways.

In our time we have seen man's chameleon capacities. We have seen a Germany turn hateful and hurtful, cruel, callous, and uncaring. And then turn again — the same people — into industrious, friendly, cheerful, rational human beings. We have witnessed the cowed behavior of southern Negroes change to the magnificent courage of the leaders for civil rights. We have watched a warring Japan — the invader of Manchuria, the pillager of China, the bomber of Pearl Harbor — write the renunciation of war into its Constitution. Italy has changed, India has changed, China has changed. Attitudes and responses, for forty years seemingly so frozen, are changing in the entire bloc of European communist countries: Yugoslavia, Rumania, Poland, Hungary, Czechoslovakia . . . .

People can be passive; or they can take their fate into their own hands.

People can be conformist and servilely obedient; or they can be questioning and individualistic.

People can be hostile or helpful, competitive or cooperative. They can be wedded to due process of law; or true believers when a leader proclaims: *"L'état, c'est moi."*

Some still say: "You can't change human nature." They continue to mouth racial and religious and national stereotypes, fixed concepts about people — "People will always be the same." The evidence is all the other way. People can be different, for better or for worse. They can sink so low, rise so high. No country is the chosen of God, the favorite of fate, the blessed of blood and genes. People are malleable. They are made and shaped by their environment and by what happens to them. The kind of human who results — the kind of society he builds — all depends . . . .

It all depends on a variety of things. On trauma, like Hiroshima. On leadership: a Kennedy, an FDR, a Mussolini or Franco. It depends on climate, on land, on resources. On the religion that holds sway. On the organization of family life. On communication — press, radio, TV, magazines, books, pamphlets, posters — and on whether or not the people have the chance to get facts. It depends on the form of government. On the heritage from the past that people carry in their minds and memories.

And: It all depends on the schools.

Schools are people factories. All schools are. Nursery schools, kindergartens, day care centers, Head Start centers . . . and all of elementary and secondary and higher general education. There are no differences here. Together we all aim at the same target: The human. We make people. People are our product.

School is the means; people are the ends. Science, mathematics, the social sciences, the humanities are the stuff through which we work; people are the ends. Puzzles, climbing apparatus, microscopes, blocks, Show-and-Tell, easels, trips: all are means, our tools. People are the ends.

A teacher of young children is not a baby-sitter, to keep children safe. She is not a jester, to keep young children smiling. Not a technician, to build little skills or little bits of knowledge in little parts of the human. A teacher of young children is more than the nurturer of maximum individual growth. A teacher helps to make society. She must know children. She must know the fields of human knowledge and wise ways of teaching them. But she must have a vision, too. She must have a dream of the good society, of the best and the most decent and the most constructive ways in which the human can function.

The Sources of a Dream

The sources of this vision are manifold. All the social sciences — history, political theory, sociology, psychology, anthropology—can contribute. All the humanities — philosophy, and ethics in partic-

ular, literature, the study of religions and of art and of music —
play a part. A good teacher must be immersed in more than Child
Development. Child Development can give us a sense of a child's
good life now. We need, too, a balancing sense of the good society,
now and for the future.

Biography can be a fount of inspiration. The lives of those we
admire can spur our thinking: prominent political figures or less
well-known men of courage . . . movers and makers of the past or
of the present . . . Americans or great leaders of the world . . .
those we admire or those who help us set our standards by their
depravity.

The landmark political documents of human advance can feed
into our dreams; proud political acts can shape our aspirations.
Philosophical and ethical and religious sources can stir our hopes.
The songs of our country and of the world, poetry and the great
novels and works of music and art all can help us know more
clearly what a good life ought to be.

Thoughtful introspection is still another source. Each of us has
had personal experiences that we treasure. We have known at firsthand a quality of human relationship that we want to see dupli-
cated more and more in the future. And each of us has seen the
mean, the petty, the destructive that we want to help wipe out.

A VISION FOR OUR FUTURE

The sources of our dreams are many. The possible answers are
many. The answers always are subjective and highly personal.

Disagreement is bound to exist. No one can presume to say:
"This is *the* answer." But everyone who teaches is duty-bound to
say: "This is *my* answer. . . . These are the precious qualities *I*
think make up the best of our country today. . . . These are *my*
dreams for an even better land tomorrow."

People Who Use Their Heads

What kind of people do we want our schools to help build, now
and for the future? Certainly boys and girls, men and women of
many qualities. But high among them: *People who use their heads.*

We need the thinking man. Knowledgeable people, with savvy. Skilled people, with know-how.

This is our American of the past, the citizen we need for tomorrow. Our country has no party line we all blindly follow, no Great White Father who tells us what to do, no Big Brother who does our thinking for us. We believe in the open marketplace of ideas. Ours is the land of the free press, the land of freedom of speech and freedom of assembly. Politically we count on rational people — people who have facts at their fingertips, who believe in getting new facts, who make up their minds on the basis of fact.

Our people, however, "vote" in more than political elections. We vote all the time. We vote in labor and business management elections. We "vote" on what to buy and how to worship, on where to live and how to travel, on the work we do and how we play, on whom our friends will be. Ours is an open society, a mobile society. We put our faith in the good sense and intelligence of the people.

Force does not decide our issues for us, neither the big issues of national life nor the day-by-day issues of personal life. Unbridled emotion should not decide for us. Propaganda, brainwashing, the big lies and little lies cannot be the basis for our decisions. The dramatic word on Harvard University's crest — *Veritas*, Truth — is a good motto for nursery schools and kindergartens, for day care centers and for Head Start, too. In a country of the people, by the people, for the people, information and know-how have a very special importance.

No child should ever go to a school that convinces him of how stupid he is — that is un-American. We want every youngster to come home from school every day with his head held higher, proud as punch, feeling smarter. Our best way of doing this is to have classrooms with the widest variety of worthwhile activities. We have to "trap" children in a classroom where no matter which way they turn there is something significant to do that challenges thinking — where there is no escape. A child learns what baby ducks are called or which stamp to put on an airmail letter — he is more knowledgeable — or he learns who treats sick animals or where the bread comes from that he buys in the store or when the ground is right for planting. He learns how to use a ruler or a magnifying glass — lucky for him, lucky for all of us, he is more

competent — or how to rollerskate or how to dial a telephone or
tie a bow or open a door with a key. He learns why snow melts
when he brings it into the classroom — he is more rational — or
why his blocks topple or why chicks take 21 days to hatch. We
need a comprehensive approach, with paths to thinking open to
all. We only have to avoid focusing too early, too narrowly on
some one royal road to competence.

Motivation Is the Key

We need people who know — and who want to know more. We
need people who are skilled — and who seek more skills. We need
people who think — and who enjoy the exercise.

In our schools the question of motivation has top priority. Our
stake is not in any specific learning as such. We need children who
like to learn and who will go on learning. We have to be leery when
they learn in school because someone makes them . . . and then
they have "had it." For us the key questions are: Why does the
child learn? Whose idea was it in the first place?

There are three broad kinds of motivation. All of them work.
Each of them has its place. Every teacher uses all three to some
extent in the course of a day. But the three are not equal. They
work out in different ways and each carries a different chain of
consequences.

There is *inherent* motivation. A child does what he does because
he loves doing it — nothing could be nicer. The activity itself is
its own reward.

There is *necessary* or *inevitable* motivation. A child does what
he does because life gives him no alternative — it is the only way
he can reach something else that he prizes. The child is not in love
with what he is doing. If he were, you would call this "inherent
motivation." But he is in love with the end-product of his activity
and there is no way around the in between step. It is not the
teacher who says he must do it — life says so. That is the way the
ball bounces. If he wants the pudding to taste right, he has to
measure the ingredients carefully; if he wants the board to fit, he
has to measure carefully — there is no way out.

There is *imposed* motivation. Here another human being is the
only motivating force. Some real-life person is the reason why the
child does what he does. The person will hurt him if he doesn't.

She will be nice if he does. The motivation is all external. The *reason why* is not in the activity itself nor in the long-range goal. A paymaster gives the reward or docks the pay. Keep your eye on that paymaster. Please her — she is the motivator.

For the future we want, inherent motivation obviously wins — hands down. When children love what they are doing, when they do it of their own accord, the chances are that they will work their hardest, learn quickest, remember longest, and that the whole learning process will become a part of them.

The chances for these good outcomes are just as promising with necessary or inevitable motivation.

But imposed motivation is a real pig in a poke. It is by all odds the trickiest. No one can be sure how it will work out. Children may work hard or they may do just as little as they think they can get away with. They may stick at what they are doing or they may daydream or giggle or roughhouse or "goof off." The only way you can be sure is to watch them very carefully. You have to keep after them and keep them on their toes. Learning is not their main goal — pleasing teacher is, or avoiding her displeasure. You have to be right on hand, alert every minute.

Even then you can't be sure. You have to stand ready to jack up the ante, to raise your prizes or increase your displeasure. The external force — "That's good work, Billy. You get a star (or a raisin or a cookie or my frown or the back of my hand)" — is the motivation. You have to adjust constantly to be sure the heat stays on.

Children may remember what they learn under imposed motivation, but you cannot bet on it. Once the teacher has been taken care of, no one can predict what will happen to the skills or facts or concepts. They are side-issues. Pleasing the teacher or avoiding her displeasure is the main business at hand. The learnings may stick. They may even last a long time. Children may be persuaded that some Big Brother is always watching them. They become afraid ever to let down, or they may go on because they can't kick the habit. But external, imposed motivation can work as easily the other way. It is a toss-up. "No one is around. Why should I?" "No one will see me. Why should I?" "It was all her idea, not mine. Now she isn't here. Why should I?" The fewest guarantees come with this kind of motivation.

The great trap of imposed motivation is that it is so frighteningly easy to use. A teacher hardly has to think — she simply has to be bigger. In the upper school the grade book and the pop-quiz and the threat of being left behind are ever-present. The teacher has the upper hand and the children know it. Woe to our future when this is the reason why children learn. But the danger is even greater with younger children. The teacher has the upper hand, and even she may not know it. The youngsters are so eager to go along, so accepting. Their eyes are so constantly on us. Every teacher of young children exerts more external force than she knows she does.

Some teachers know the power they have and they rationalize their use of it. There is the great temptation to think about young children: They need someone big to tell them, someone big to show them, someone big to make them. Unfortunately, no rationalization changes the way the odds work out. Use imposed motivation and no one can tell what the chances are. The child may remember or he may not. The child may continue learning or he may not. The child may enjoy the process or he may not.

A wise school does well to play the game the safest, surest way. It strives for inherent motivation or for that reasonable facsimile thereof, necessary or inevitable motivation. It does not make this choice for romantic reasons, to be "nice" to little children. Nor does it deny that life is full of many things we all have to do, whether we like them or not. The reliance on sound motivation is hardheaded realism. Learning is too important a business to take a chance on. There is so much for children to learn today and there will be even more for them to learn tomorrow. We have to use the safest motivation just as much as we can. It is the only sure way of producing people who use their heads, who like to use their heads, who learn because learning is their own idea.

Any nursery school, kindergarten, day care, or Head Start program fails its children — and all of us — if its youngsters end the day on a plateau having learned nothing new. They fail their children—and all of us—if the youngsters end the day with their tails between their legs having learned that they cannot do what is expected. They fail their children — and all of us — if the youngsters end the day having learned many skills and facts and concepts but always under a motivation that lets closure quickly set in: "Learning is for the birds . . . we have had it!"

People Who Are Rugged Individualists

What kind of people do we want our schools to help build? *Rugged individualists* ought to be another prized target.

Our schools ought to be distinctively committed to nurturing initiative, imagination, drive. They ought to be wedded to the development of resourcefulness and independence and ingenuity.

Ours has been a "can-do" land: "The difficult we do immediately, the impossible takes a little longer." Proudly we have proclaimed: "You can't keep a good man down." We are a nation of "good men," people with creativity and guts.

This spirit has brought us our high standard of living and all our material comforts. We joke about Horatio Alger but Horatio has innumerable real-life counterparts — people who had an idea, who took a chance, who moved ahead. Through all the years people have tried to dream up a better mousetrap so the world would beat a path to their door. The "mousetrap" has turned out to be a cotton gin, an elevator, automobiles, computers, farm equipment, typewriters, refrigerators, pens. . . .

Our whole life, not only our economic life, bears this adventuresome stamp. Our land was settled by "can-do" people who conquered a rockbound coast. We are the people who crossed the Donner Pass, who dammed the raging Tennessee, the people who built the Panama Canal, the people of the Berlin Airlift, who built those thousands of Liberty Ships for World War II. "They" said "it" couldn't be done, so Americans — smart, yes, but ingenious and inventive more so — found a new way of doing it.

Fortunately the Jonas Salks are in our tradition as much as the Daniel Boones. Our better world of tomorrow will not only come through the production of more goods and chattels alone. The future lies in the imaginative solution to basic problems of living: taming the city, farming the sea, finding more drinking water, purifying the air, conquering crippling and killing diseases, controlling the weather, building greater sensitivity in human relationships. Yesterday's Americans did not wait for "George" to do it. Tomorrow's Americans must be activists, too. We need a continuing flow of innovators, of originators.

All the components of creativity are far from being known. But at least three elements of free-floating thinking stand out. These three — *curiosity, ego-strength, absorption* — ought to be among our most prized targets.

Curiosity

Our schools must foster the probing, wondering mind. They must be schools full of surprises, full of mystery. We must do our best to nurture the openness of people, their sense of awareness, their responsiveness to the life around them. Schools that promote curiosity search out the eye-catching picture, never settling for stereotyped reproduction of ordinary everyday life: mother, father, a kitten, a glass of milk, "cute" baby chicks. They seek arresting displays, not content with the staid and mundane that no child ever notices. We must keep feeding into our classrooms new pieces of equipment, new juxtapositions of the novel and the familiar so that school life never becomes old hat, the same old thing. We must weed out the drab, all the dull routines of education: the boring sit-in-a-circle attendance-taking every morning, the monotony of everlasting Show-and-Tell. We have no stake in classrooms where one day is dismally like every other, all drearily the same.

Our goal should be to get children to use one form of sentence structure more and more: *the question.* "What is that?" "What is it for?" "What can you do with it?" "Where did it come from?" "What is it made of?" "Why is it that way?" — these must be our children's refrains. And the answers must come, not through our words alone, but through children using their fingers, noses, their eyes and ears, the tips of their tongues to taste. Questions must also be the teacher's main stock in trade: "What do you think?" "What is your guess?" "How can you find out?" The American school must be a school for excited discovery.

Ego-Strength

We need to nurture uniqueness and independence just as strongly. Ours must be schools for ego-strength — the child's ego, not the teacher's. "You can do it!" has to be the teacher's consistent, over-and-over steady slogan: "You can hang up your own coat" . . . "You can pour your own juice" . . . "You can climb to the top" . . . "You can figure it out."

We have no stake in schools where children learn to color within the lines. No stake in pushing for unnecessary conformity, no stake in children submerging themselves in the group, no stake in everlasting lessons in obediently following directions: "Draw a line . . . ," "Make a mark . . . ," "Circle the one . . . ." The youngster whose ways are different ought to excite our attention, not our angry determination to make him fit in.

We want our youngsters to learn to take a chance, to go out on their personal limb. We want them to try — and not to suffer too-painful penalties if their way is not our way. Fortunately early education is blessed with time-tested equipment and supplies that are "mistake-free." Many commonly used materials are designed purposefully so that there is no one specific right or wrong way to proceed. A child cannot go wrong with easel or finger painting — there is no possible way to make a "mistake." There is no right or wrong way in dramatic play, in the housekeeping corner or on the jungle gym or outdoors on tricycles or in blockbuilding or wherever play takes place. There is no "wrong" way with clay or collage or sand or water activity. There are only right ways, hundreds of right ways, each child's way. An American school should glory in these open-ended opportunities. Let the cultures that prize uniformity, conformity, passivity stock their schools with supplies and equipment designed to make children hew to a line.

The distinctive characteristic of play is that the rules are all in the child's mind. Play builds the kind of free-and-easy, try-it-out, do-it-yourself character that our future needs. We must become more self-conscious and more explicit in our praise and reenforcement as children use unstructured play materials: "That's good. You used your own ideas" . . . "That's good. You did it your way" . . . "That's good. You thought it all out yourself."

Children's play has never been well understood by many adults; it is, dangerously, under attack more now than in the past. There is pressure to cut out dramatic play or to treat it as dramatics — a performance. The child is assigned a role: "Be Little Red Riding Hood" or "Be one of the Three Little Pigs." The child becomes an actor, not a creator. There is pressure to turn painting into a time for lessons: "Draw a turkey and make it look the way a turkey should" ... "Draw a tree and color it green" ... "Draw a house and put all the windows in." Finger paint and sand and water play are skimped — they are too messy. Clay is tolerated, but too often the goal is for the child to make an ash tray for Mother's Day.

Puzzles have prestige today, and form boards and peg boards — there is a right and wrong way of using them. Games are the outdoor rage: London Bridge, Statues, Follow the Leader .... The rules for the games don't originate with the children; the youngsters simply follow the rules. Achievement is becoming our number one goal: "Do you know your colors?" ... "Can you say the alphabet?" ... "Do you know some finger plays?" We must beware lest we end up with the wrong kind of achievement. In the push for a finished puzzle we don't want to lose a confident human who has the capacity to come through with something novel — he could be our proudest achievement.

Absorption

America needs schools for absorption, as well as schools for curiosity and ego-strength. We should want our children to throw themselves into what they are doing, to lose themselves in what they are doing, to be so involved that they become oblivious to much that is around them. We cannot avoid all interruptions of intense, personal drive. Of course, we will always have to say: "It's time for our trip" . . . "It's time to go home." But we must be leery of needlessly interrupting the enthusiast. We want to nurture the passion that young children bring to their personal choices. As much as we can, we have to guard against cutting off the child who is lost in his work: "It's time to clean up now" . . . "It's time for everyone to come to music" . . . "It's time for everyone to come hear a story."

We are not after the all-around hack-of-all-trades. There is no point in saying: "You painted yesterday. Work with clay today" ... "You have been at the workbench for two days now. You have to try something else before you can go back." True: There are dangers if fear or lack of skill hold a child in some uncomfortable rut. But there are no dangers — to the child or to any of us — if a youngster freely chooses and persists because the activity is important to him. This is the kind of personal conviction we have to cherish.

If we can make our classrooms provocative of curiosity, appreciative of uniqueness, respectful of passion and devotion and drive, we will do our children a favor — and we do a favor for the future, too.

People with a Heart

What kind of people do we want our schools to help build? Certainly also: *People with a heart.*

We seek the decent human being. Compassionate. Generous. Kind. Sympathetic. Friendly. Helpful. Cooperative. America needs people who care, people who are utterly repelled by cruelty, meanness, the petty hurtful ways of life.

Our religions have been saying to us through the years: *Do unto others as you would have them do unto you.* We have moved slowly but steadily toward this end in our domestic political life. Our freeing of the slaves, our child labor and minimum wage laws and laws governing working hours, social security, unemployment insurance, welfare and old age assistance, our civil rights legislation, Medicare — all have been steps along the way.

Internationally we have been a nation with a helping hand. We have been at our best developing the Marshall Plan and in our continuing efforts at foreign aid, in our contributions to UNICEF, in the Peace Corps, and the other humanitarian efforts of the United Nations today. We have caused our share of suffering, but suffering repels us. When we are true to ourselves we try to make amends.

A strand in our living — one we should want to nurture — puts us on the side of the underdog. So strong a country, one so lucky in escaping man-made and natural disasters, could easily live in isolation. We could enjoy our blessings and let the devil take the hindmost. Instead we have given generously, as individuals and as a nation, to flood relief and fire relief, to hurricane and earthquake and tornado relief, to famine relief. We have been aware, we must become more aware: No man is an island . . . all men are brothers. Our basic position was stated at the time of our founding — an unusual statement in public affairs: All men have the right to life, liberty, *and the pursuit of happiness.* Americans look on life as good to live, not a travail to suffer through in pain, sorrow, and despair.

An American can be touched, he can be reached. Our schools must help keep our people that way.

Today's young children are headed, beyond any shadow of doubt, toward an increasingly interdependent world. The speed of transportation, the ease of communication, the interlacing of economies, the ever-present threat of universal destruction make this world one shrinking planet, one tight family of man. For children's self-protection the capacity to care — for people we know, people we have never seen; for people like us, people very different; for people near at hand and those far out of sight — must be nurtured. For children's self-fulfillment, so that they can grow into the deepest potential of their humanity, this sense of caring must be ever nurtured.

Children learn to care by experiencing good care. They come to know the blessings of gentleness, of sympathy, of patience and kindness, of support and backing first through the way in which they themselves are treated. This is a reason why young children need teachers who have the personal touch. They need a teacher who will come to see them when they are at home because of illness. They need a teacher who sometime will call them up at the end of the day — a person-to-person call directly to the child — simply to say "Hello" or to praise him for something he has done well.

Not all children are so lucky as to experience these blessings in school. Few teachers set out to be mean to youngsters. Many, however, manage to be very, very busy. Many more build rationalizations for actions that children can only interpret as rebuffs. We think our heart is in the right place when we say that we don't want children to be cry babies or mama's babies or to think they can get their way by whimpering. Many a youngster looking for a helping hand gets a cold shoulder instead: "Don't come running to me with every little hurt." We can succeed in teaching children that they cannot count on people — they are not around when you need them, they won't help you if they are around; or we can truly succeed in the opposite way.

Children learn to care by seeing others treated well. They need to learn that people matter most of all. Many youngsters escape petty meanness themselves but they see others bear the brunt: "We've had just about enough out of you" . . . "If you want to cry, cry in the corner but don't bother the rest of us." Children hear sarcasm when they should hear sensitivity. They see others shamed when they should see others helped. They see children picked on who should be picked up. They see boys and girls isolated who need most of all to be included. American youngsters need to live with the Good Samaritan. Many do, of course. More must, if we are to produce gentle people.

But too many learn that the thing to do is to ignore the less fortunate or take advantage of them: "We can't wait all day for Johnny." It is so easy for classrooms to have a scapegoat. It is so easy to spotlight the unpopular minorities, the children whom it is legitimate and safe to pick on. Children hear others labeled: Slow-poke . . . Bully . . . Show-off . . . Cry baby . . . . These are the people we don't have to care about. But the victims are not the only ones hurt—the strong and the lucky learn a little callousness.

Suffusing a classroom with sensitivity, so that each child experiences it and sees all others experience it too, is a challenge that must be met at every point in a day, not only in some "social studies" time when we talk about the policeman who is our friend and the fireman who is our helper. The lessons of friendliness and helpfulness must emerge from playtime and worktime, from toilet-ing and juice time, from music and science, indoors and out, from the routines and the transitions. The teacher's personal relation-ships with each and every child must be the best exemplification of good nature and good nurture that one can imagine.

Children's relationships one with the other are also of first-rate importance. A child must come to feel that people make life go better. At this early stage in social growth a youngster can easily come to think: "People are a problem" . . . "You always have to stop for people, you always have to wait for them, you never can do what you want to because of people." The group — society — can seem like a hindrance: "People are not a joy, they are a nuisance."

This negative outcome is more likely whenever children are forced into a society that is larger than they can cope with. Young children easily like people if there are not too many of them. They do beautifully any time they can operate on a face-to-face, one-to-one basis. They do beautifully any time they can work in small groups of two or three or four. But jump this social beginner up into a larger crowd and strain can set in. Schools concerned about children learning to care must be very cautious about all the mass-meeting times: Show-and-Tell, planning times, story time, music time, evaluation time. We must be very skeptical about the coliseum gatherings of young children: the all-school assemblies, the field days, all-school movies. There is nothing our society can gain by teaching children to exist side-by-side but in isolation.

We must be especially on guard against competition in young children's groups. It is so tempting to pit children one against the other: "The girls are quiet. We're waiting for the boys" . . . "Billy is standing up nice and straight and quiet but we're waiting for the rest of you." Competition works in some instances at some ages, but forced competition can not work to teach young children that we have to live together.

People Who Are Free

What kind of people do we want our schools to help build? *A free people.* An American school ought to be especially full of the joys of liberty, the joys of openness, the joys of movement and of choice and of fluidity.

Ours is the land of liberty. The desire for freedom led the first settlers to our shore. It brought our country its waves of later immigration. It was the motive behind our westward migration. Freedom was the rallying cry of our first revolution and remains the cry of our continuing revolutions: "Freedom now!" for labor, for women, for racial minorities . . . . Freedom was the first demand following our revolution, and was buttressed in our Bill of Rights. It continues as a persisting concern today as our courts defend the concept of due process of law. We have known freedom in our religious life and we have woven it into the whole fabric of our social life. Americans do not kowtow to titled power, to moneyed power, to traditional power. We have no fear of police power, no fear of the state itself.

Ours is the land of the free. It will continue to be, if our schools are freedom-full today.

No young child ought to go to our schools to learn to feel scared. At their age freedom has an at-ease air. It does not hold with standing in line, standing at attention. Freedom has an informal, casual air. It becomes polluted by groups moving en masse. Freedom has an air of jollity, a happy buzz. The lid is not clamped down by force or sweetness. Freedom has an openness in human relationships. No inner or outer censor curbs every thought and action.

In a freedom-full school choice is respected, choice is encouraged. Children choose their friends — playmates and workmates are not assigned. Children choose their work — it is not forced on them. They have freedom of movement. A child can stay with his easel or book or workbench or puzzle, even though all the others work on something else. In a free setting a child feels safe to be a minority; he does not feel guilty or tense, offbeat or oddball, because he does not go along with the crowd.

One tipoff on the extent of freedom is how young children look at their teacher. A teacher is authority, but free men are not afraid of authority. Nor do they stand aloof from authority keeping a cool, calculating, suspicious distance, a you-go-your-way-and-I'll-go-my-way kind of distance.

Youngsters are close to their teacher — they love her — in a freedom-full school. They think she is the most wonderful person in the whole wide world. She could win a popularity contest with them any time, not because she lets them get away with murder but because she is understanding. She is firm when she has to be, a critic when she has to be, but she is gentle. She stops children when she has to, but she never undercuts a child. Most of all, a teacher is around when the children need her: sympathetic, supporting, interested, boosting, helpful. Youngsters know they can count on her. She is on the child's side and the child knows it, just as in a free society the state and government are for the people.

In a freedom-full school painful punishments are out. Yelling at children is out. Shaming children, embarrassing them, is out.

License and anarchy are out, too. A good school cannot be a school for life in the jungle or for a dog-eat-dog society. Ours is a land of liberty but it is a land of law. We do not want a policeman at every corner but we do want a conscience in every heart. A good school works for excellent discipline but its methods fit the discipline of free people.

Rules Are Right for the Age

There are rules but the rules are right for the age. The rules fit active, busy, moving children. Laws that unnecessarily say "Sit" to such youngsters could not lead to discipline; they would only make criminals of the children, or cowed people if the youngsters did not fight back. The rules and regulations fit talking, social children. Laws that say "Shush" would only teach them to be bad, or resentful if the children gave in. Laws that call for too much waiting, for too much all-coming-together-as-a-group, for not-touching, for playing-the-game-the-"right"-way would teach neither liberty nor respect for authority. They would play a part in undercutting the future we want. Good laws are tuned to children as they are now, not as they some day will be.

Rules Are Not Arbitrary

There are rules but the rules are not arbitrary. Children are helped to understand why the rules have to be, what their logic is, the good they serve. A teacher of young children is everlastingly making a case for decency and for appropriate behavior. This is a time-consuming process. It is essentially a talking, reasoning process. It is the slow, steady, bit-by-bit business of helping a child see the sense of acting in a certain way. The teacher says the case; she talks it through; she discusses it. Finally the reason and the law sink into the child and become his reason and his law. Rules and regulations are not imposed by a Caesar or a Franco, by a vague and distant City Hall, or by some all-powerful Party. As a free man — a young free man — the child accepts the limitation as his own. The laws make sense to him.

In a freedom-full school for the young there is no place for "Because I tell you so" . . . "Because I say so." *I* — I am bigger than you, I am stronger than you — *I*, the Marines, the occupying force, the Gestapo. The free man, even the very young free man, understands and accepts the law because the case for decency appeals to him. He doesn't obey merely because he is small and overrun.

There is no place for "*WE* don't throw sand" or "*WE* don't run outside the fence." The rule is right but the reason is wrong. The free man is not a conformist — "*WE* don't throw blocks" because no one else does—nor is he a herd-follower—"I do throw blocks" because everyone else does. He is good because he wants to be good and sees the point in being good.

Punishments Are Not Cruel or Inhuman

There are rules but there are no cruel and inhuman punishments. Slapping children, pinching children, yanking children, tying them into their chairs, dunce caps, and "bad chairs" all occur too often. They should never happen. Nor should the yell across the room, the furious scowl, the threatening tone. Our young children should grow up unhurt by law enforcement, not hurt physically or psychologically, no matter what their "crime."

Laws will be broken, even sound and appropriate ones. Laws are broken on Main Street. They are bound to be broken in groups for sheer beginners. Young children have a lot to learn and discipline takes a long time to learn. Broken laws should be no surprise, but a good teacher is not casual about broken laws nor does she simply shrug off the infraction.

The laws of a free society must ultimately be obeyed. Education cannot teach that authority is a pushover or that laws are made to be flouted. No youngster must ever have the cheap, shoddy feeling that he is "getting away with it." No youngster must ever learn the tyrannical sense that he is above the law. No matter how long it takes, no matter how persistently the teacher must work at it, the law must be obeyed in the long run.

A society is at its worst when it becomes a land of lawlessness. There can only be shame at crime in the streets. The same distress should be felt when there are little "crimes" in the nursery school, the kindergarten, the day care center, or Head Start. A society pays far too great a price for lawlessness to be "permissive" or untroubled about its early beginnings.

When a law is broken, however, the solution is seldom a simple-minded one: a scream or a blow. Any twelve-year-old could do that. Squelching a symptom may bring a moment's peace now but it is the feeblest guarantee of peace in the years to come. The prevention of delinquency is a complex matter, not some easy little problem that brute force or a loud voice can quickly solve. It takes the best thinking of a wise and sensitive teacher.

When a law is broken such a teacher faces one immediate question: *Why?* Why did the child do it? A good teacher has to be a detective, not to find the culprit but to find the cause. Her nose starts to twitch, her ears stand up straight, her brain and heart begin to churn. *Why?* Maybe the law itself is a bad one, one that ought to be repealed. Maybe the child does not yet fully understand the law; the solution may come through more patient, calm, reasonable interpretation. Maybe the child understands and knows full well how he ought to act, but maybe he is driven by compulsive needs that ride herd over his knowledge. Then the solution should not be more reasoning but an earnest effort to identify those unmet needs and do something to meet them. Maybe hunger is the real villain. Or fatigue. Or some physical difficulty. Maybe . . . maybe . . . . There are many possible answers and they are difficult to uncover. But a teacher committed to freedom knows that she has to get to the cause. Her goal is not simply to control a child, to make him good in school. She wants a child who will be good all through his life, because he makes himself act that way. She seeks to build a child who knows the right thing to do, who feels good about it, and who willingly acts that way.

Other Prized Qualities

What kind of people do we want our schools to help build? There could be items five, six, seven, eight, and still more in any one person's dream.

Some might say: *We need people with a sense of humor.* Certainly our country, in particular, should prize gaiety, laughter, the lifting light touch. Life in the U.S.A. should never be sullen, sodden, soggy, a plodding existence. Our days should sparkle.

Some might say: *Aesthetes.* We should work to develop a keen appreciation of beauty in our people: the beauty in nature, in manmade products, beauty in human relationships. Ours ought to be a land where good taste pervades, where people live in cultivated high style.

Some might say: *People with vitality and vigor.* Our boys and girls should build grace, nimbleness, strength. They should be housed in bodies that are a joy to live in, a joy for others to see. Today's young children will live a very long time and they should live their lengthened span in glowing health.

Some might say: *Men and women of courage* — the brave physically, and those who will dare to stand up for their convictions.

Some: *Men and women who take pride in their work.*

Some: *Leaders.* People skilled in getting the best out of others.

Some might seek to build *those who will thrive on differences.* In the past our country has been the world's melting pot. In our children's future the wide world itself will be a melting pot. Children can be taught to feel that differences make life exciting, alluring, rich. They can be helped to build a positive taste for variety: in skin color and customs, in interests and abilities, variety in sights and sounds and smells.

The kind of people our schools help to build all depends . . . .

It all depends on teachers who will dream, and then translate their dreams into reality within their classrooms. They don't wait. They build the good society *now* . . . immediately . . . right within the four walls of their room. They work consistently so that, from the very beginning, children live the good life, love the good life, and carry it with them in their bloodstream on into tomorrow. The good society is not in the future — it starts today.

Thinking and Planning Together

Teachers, of course, must mesh their dreams with parents' dreams. We have to think and plan together. This is especially imperative in the under-six age range where half-day sessions of school are so common. The half-day impact is a very tiny impact unless what happens at school is reenforced and extended and deepened at home. One must pick up where the other leaves off, and both must move in the same direction.

Impact almost vanishes when home and school work at cross-purposes. Too many children are caught in a cross fire. One of their "schools" teaches conformity, the other works for creativity. One prizes blind obedience while the other seeks to install critical thinking. One says "Turn the other cheek" — the other urges "Stand up for your rights." One deprecates a given behavior as tattling; the other rewards the same behavior as social awareness. One relies on force, the other on reason. The child caught in such a tangle of values all too often is indecisive and uncommitted. His home learnings and his school learnings have fought each other.

We have to end the separation of home and school. Too much is at stake to let the foolish lack of communication persist in which the left hand never knows what the right hand is doing.

Head Start has taken a strong hand on the need for parents and teachers working together, hand in glove. It recognizes that the corrosive effects of poverty can only be undone through a twenty-four hour attack. The need is no less pressing in nursery school, kindergarten, or the day care center. The prod of poverty is missing but the problem is the same. Children do not get a fair deal — our whole society suffers — unless school and home consciously strive together to build the human we both want.

We must get together in markedly better ways than we do.

At present so much time is wasted on unimportant business details. So much time goes to fringe matters. So much time is spent on generalities, far from the central issue of how these three- and four- and five-year-olds should spend their life now. Too often we are simply going through the motions. Too many meetings merely let parents chalk one up — they have been "good" parents and have dutifully gone to a meeting. Too many meetings merely let teachers sigh a sigh of relief — they have been "good" teachers and have met with parents. But nothing is accomplished, and no one has any expectations of accomplishment.

It is time for a change.

Teachers of young children have to meet in their own rooms with their children's own parents: no outside speakers, no froufrou, no folderol.

These room meetings have to center on the crucial questions that these immediate co-workers face. Nothing could be more crucial than discussion of the kind of person we want to build. What are the qualities we prize? What do we want to emerge from our joint efforts? What are we after? And what are the appropriate ways of achieving our goal?

There are bound to be differences at first. The quick answer, the partial answer, the short-term answer is very appealing: Someone who minds, someone who does his work .... But we have to keep on meeting and keep on talking and keep hammering away — one meeting once a month may not do the trick.

We are talking about young Americans. Barring personal or national tragedy, these boys and girls will live well past the year 2000. They will live in a century when man will be even more the master of his environment. What kind of Man do we want these boys and girls to be? And what kind of environment do we want them to build? These questions cannot be postponed for the agenda of college parents and teachers or for the high school team. The future human and the future society are built, in part, by the way boys and girls live in the nursery school, the kindergarten, the day care center, and Head Start. Parents and teachers of young children have to think through their answers now.

4

A Subject-Matter Centered Program

People always say: "Schools should teach the 3 R's." There is no question about it. Schools must. Nursery schools must. Kindergartens, day care centers, Head Start . . . all schools must.

There is no necessary conflict between this concern and the goal of under-six education to help children live their third, fourth, and fifth years of life at the peak of their powers. There is no conflict between it and the goals of a democratic school: to develop rugged individualists, free men, boys and girls who will use their heads and have a heart.

The term — the 3 R's — is, of course, only shorthand — a quickie way of saying "human knowledge." We use this shorthand more in elementary education. Colleges have their own way of grouping knowledge, a much broader and more comprehensive label. Colleges teach the Liberal Arts. They teach the Humanities, Mathematics and the Sciences, the Social Sciences, Health and Physical Education.

Nursery schools must teach the Liberal Arts too. And so must kindergartens, day care centers, Head Start.

SUBJECT MATTER IN THE SCHOOL

The job of any school for general education is to teach all the subject matters. Other institutions—libraries, museums, hospitals, recreation centers, neighborhood centers — work through their particular areas of specialty. Subject matter is the school's baili-wick. We have to teach subject matter — there is nothing else for us to work through.

You can use the shorthand symbol for knowledge: the 3 R's. You can use the broader heading: the Liberal Arts. You can start with A and go on down the list to Z and specify each subject matter. A school — nursery school, kindergarten, day care, Head Start, elementary, secondary, general college — must teach them all:

Anthropology	English	Mathematics
Arithmetic	Foreign Languages	Music
Art	Geology	Philosophy
Astronomy	Government and Politics	Physics
Biology	Home Economics	Psychology
Chemistry	Health	Reading
Civics	History	Sociology
Economics	Literature	Zoology

The teacher of young children cannot simply be child centered. She must be child centered, society centered, *and* tuned in on culture, on knowledge. She must be a broadly educated, well-informed person. Her "professional" training is not simply the pedagogical preparation that helps her understand children and the techniques of teaching them. Her own liberal arts background is a fundamental part of her professional training. When you teach young children you teach with all you know — and with all you can find out — about all the fields of study.

For years there has been a common assumption: "Anyone can teach young children. All a nursery school or kindergarten teacher has to know is how to mix the paints." This misconception is spreading today because of the rapid expansion of the field. The resulting severe teacher shortage means that many are being hired whose own cultural backgrounds are limited. High school gradu-ates, those with one or two years of college study, junior college graduates suddenly become "teachers."

Even before today's great teacher shortage, not all nursery-kindergarten teachers were "brains," in the academic sense of the word. Many had intuitive psychological understandings that made them very skilled in human relationships and very sensitive to children. Some of today's "new teachers" are equally gifted in empathy. Some understand children's poverty backgrounds well, some speak the language of the poor. These are great strengths. But young children will suffer if early education always has to choose: Be sensitive *or* be smart . . . Be kind *or* be informed . . . Be gentle *or* be wise.

Smart teachers, bright teachers, informed teachers, cultured teachers are needed by young children, every bit as much as older youngsters need them. The good teaching of young children requires a rounded background, rich in psychological insights, rich in democratic awareness, *and* equally rich in cultural attainment. Facts and concepts and skills must be taught. They must be taught starting at age three, not postponed until some later time.

The Ways of Teaching Differ

The crux lies in how subject matter is taught. To say that subject matter is the business of under-six education does not mean that the nursery school, kindergarten, day care center or Head Start program will look and sound the same as the upper grades. The same fields of study are taught but: *The ways of teaching are different.* This is a very fundamental difference.

The methods of teaching young children are not new or radical, not revolutionary or unheard-of. They are all methods used with older students, too. But some of the methods have a much higher priority in under-six education — they are used much more extensively than in the grades. And some of the old standard methods are used very little with young children. *The heart of the difference is in balance and in proportion.* This shifting of the weight can make the good under-six class seem deceptively offbeat to anyone who only knows the education of older children. It can make it seem as if subject matter is not being taught. The subject matter has to be there, even though the difference in the balance and proportion of teaching methods may seem to hide it.

The teacher of young children lectures at times to the whole class — but very seldom and very briefly.

She has recitation periods and question-and-answer sessions — but these are rare.

She leads all-group discussions — but infrequently.

The most widely used of all the talking-teaching techniques are face-to-face, person-to-person lessons. This is tutoring, under-six style.

All in all, however, the teacher of young children does not talk a great deal. Her relatively few words carry great weight, if she uses them properly. But the under-six teacher relies much more heavily on other teaching methods.

The teacher of young children encourages youngsters to work alone. This is independent study and it has high priority.

She emphasizes committee work, too. This is a standard teaching technique at all age levels but one that has high priority with young children. Under-six "committees" are all exceedingly informal and short-lived. They have a changing membership, self-chosen. The members seldom sit down to meet; these are working committees. But a major part of a teacher's skill lies in making it possible for young children to learn from each other.

She teaches to some extent through books and movies and slides and filmstrips and tape recorders and bulletin boards and pictures and many other kinds of audiovisual aids to learning, as all teachers do.

The strongest emphasis in under-six education, however, is the laboratory approach. Or call it field study. The teacher's biggest job is to take children to where the action is or to bring the action in to them. She tries continually to confront her youngsters with experiences, with events. She looks for significant situations in which the children can be actively involved. The teacher of young children seeks *Happenings*.

A Happening is always a verb. When the children are baking or buying or cooking or playing or painting or digging or washing or making or selling — this is a Happening. Science is not a Happening. Mathematics is not a Happening. Nor are the units found so often in kindergartens and in some nursery schools: The Seasons, Transportation, The Home, The Farm .... These are all nouns. Young children need verbs. Events. Action.

Small wonder that some people think that anyone can teach young children. A good teacher of the young does not look like a "teacher." You seldom find her up in front of the class — she is in the middle of the action. The children don't sit all day — they are up and around, busy and involved, doing things. The teacher does not rely on books, textbooks, or workbooks. She concentrates on experiences in which the youngsters can participate. Happenings come first — they are basic.

Subject-Matter Labels

The teacher teaches subject matter but the subject-matter labels are primarily in her mind. They do not show on the outside. The teacher thinks in terms of mathematics, science, reading . . . . The children cook or plant or build a house. Inside her mind the teacher pinpoints the facts and concepts and skills that lie embedded in the experiences. But the daily program only shows and the children can only tell about the Happening: They are digging a garden, they are feeding the birds, they are going to the shoe repair shop. An alert teacher can pull the subject-matter learnings out of any significant activity; but the activity has to be going on in the first place for her to do her job.

Keeping the subject-matter labels in the background, putting the focus on experience, is not a drastic step. We must not let these labels awe us. They are for the teacher's convenience. The labels are all man-made; we have thought them up ourselves and we keep changing them from time to time. Today we speak of the Language Arts in the elementary school. You seldom find that label used in high schools or colleges. At those levels we speak of Speech or Creative Writing or Literature or Composition. Civics is a common label in junior and senior high school. The same subject matter is called Government and Politics in college. The elementary school teaches the Social Studies. Colleges label each of the specifics: History, Government, Economics, Sociology, Anthropology . . . .

Through the years some once-popular headings have disappeared. Theology once was a central field in general education; today it is a part of professional training. We add on new subject-matter labels as the years go along. Once there was only the label

Biology. Now there are many subdivisions: Anatomy, Taxonomy, Cytology, Embryology, Ecology, Histology, Paleontology, Teratology . . . .

The labels are simply administrative devices. They did not come from heaven and they do not exist in reality. No real-life event ever is limited to one label or one subject matter. Life comes in big bundles, with the contents all mixed up. Experiences never can be neatly compartmentalized.

A group of four-year-olds takes a trip to a farm to learn where milk comes from. If you make the teacher put one label on the experience she will probably have to call it Science. Or if that isn't specific enough: Biology. Or if that is still too general: Animal Biology. But what about all the conversation that goes on in connection with the trip: before, during, after? That should be called the Language Arts. The stories before and after the trip are Literature. The singing — "Old MacDonald Had a Farm" is fated to be sung! — must be called Music. Rules for conduct are developed. This is what Civics and Government and Politics are all about. The teacher recalls what happened the last time the group took a trip: "You remember how we all crowded around and some people could not see." The lessons of the past are usually labeled History. A child misbehaves; the teacher's response is a lesson in Psychology. Someone counts the children to be sure no one is left at the farm: Arithmetic. The trip costs money; the minute that question comes up the four-year-olds take a brief course in Economics. The cow is probably pretty, even if the farmer and the highway are not. The presence of beauty and the absence of it are matters of Aesthetics. When the teacher soothes a disappointed child — "Things don't always work out the way we want" — the lesson is one in Philosophy. And hopefully on such a trip the children drink some milk — that experience is labeled Nutrition! Yet the whole trip was labeled Science!

The best place for the labels is in the teacher's mind. Knowing the organization of knowledge helps her focus on what there is for her to teach. But the children do not have to sit down to learn subject matter. They do not have to keep quiet to learn subject matter. They do not have to stay together as a whole group to learn subject matter. They do not have to read subject matter out of a book. And the label does not have to show.

STIMULUS

Under-six and over-six education share the same general flow and pattern of instruction — there is no difference here. The first job of all schools is to confront children with rich stimulation. We must all provide yeast, a starter that will make children's minds stretch, their bodies stretch, that will deepen their social awareness and widen their emotional responses. Stimulation is the reason why children, no matter what their age, come to school. They must sink their teeth into something meaty or they might just as well stay home.

In all education this flood tide of stimulus is followed by a second stage: ample and generous time for response. Three-year-old students, thirteen-year-old students need the chance to react to the stimulus, to organize their own impressions and sensations, to incorporate inside of themselves all that has flowed in. First stimulus, then response — this is the standard pattern of education.

Colleges provide stimulation through top-flight lectures. Colleges and all the upper levels of education open up new vistas through books: "Read the next ten pages" .... "the next chapter" .... "the books in the bibliography." Movies — documentaries, teaching films — can provide the initial ferment for older children.

Teachers of young children start with reality.

In the beginning, for boys and girls who have not been to school before, the sheer fact of school is itself stimulating. School is a stimulus simply because it exists — it is "there." This — for three-year-olds, for new fours and fives, for Head Start children — is a great challenge. The new setting, the companionship of children, the wide array of indoor and outdoor equipment are a rich feast.

This initial impact is like that of a campus on the college freshman. The buildings, the grounds, the statues, the traditions, the dorms, the student union, the library, the new freedom and new responsibilities, the songs, the football games, roommates, professors, the style of dress — there is so much to take in. Every sight and sound, every personality, every location starts wheels churning. In the same way the well-equipped classroom for the very young, filled with the right materials and with children, provides the initial flood tide of sensation, impression, challenge, invitation — as much as beginners can take.

The Many Faces of a Teacher

The teacher does a major part of her teaching before the children ever come to school by setting the scene so that it is stimulating. No one sees the teacher do this. Small wonder again that there is that rumor that anyone can teach young children! Yet making this initial stimulation right for the children who come is skilled work.

The teacher must be an astute purchaser. It is costly to equip a laboratory for young children, just as it is costly to equip a science laboratory or a business education or home economics education laboratory. A skilled teacher exercises very selective judgment in what she buys and what she passes by.

She especially needs a highly developed sales resistance. Workbooks are promoted which have zero-stimulation value and inappropriate response value for children at this age. Active sales campaigns promote overly expensive kits, especially ones allegedly designed for Head Start children, which have more attractive packaging than contents. It is easy to spend a disproportionate part of a budget on high-priced equipment which offers only minimal return in stimulation and in opportunity for child response. Big sums can be wasted on expensive swings, on fancy merry-go-rounds, on elaborate overhead and motion picture projectors. Money can be wasted on materials which are not sturdy enough to stand up to hard use by a group of active children.

A teacher who is a wise spender looks primarily for materials that are "unstructured." She wants open-ended materials that can be used in many different ways for the countless purposes that children themselves think up. In the indoor classroom the sets of unit blocks, the easels and paints and clay, tubs and water tables, the materials for dramatic play, the small boats and cars and figures of people and animals, the dolls and doll carriages, workbench materials all meet this standard. In the outdoor classroom large blocks, boards and boxes and ladders, climbing apparatus, tricycles and wheel toys, the sandbox are similarly unstructured.

These are multi-purpose materials — they promote intellectual and social and physical growth. And they are double-edged: These are stimulus materials and materials for children's response.

Some needed equipment is structured. Young children need a generous supply of books. They need many puzzles, peg boards and form boards of varying difficulty. They need phonograph records of high quality. Our classrooms also need as many as possible and appropriate of the special tools that the various fields of learning use.

Typically under-six education has done exceedingly well in providing good tools in one field: art. A classroom for young children often looks for all the world like an artist's studio. The products that come out are children's products but the process that goes on is the artist's process. The rich availability of easels, paints, brushes, paper, clay, collage materials helps young children live like artists, feel like artists.

Our classrooms must be equally rich in the tools of all the Liberal Arts. Instruments for measurement, for example, are central to mathematics. Instruments for observation are basic to all the sciences. We want our children to act and feel like three-year-old, four-year-old, five-year-old scholars in many fields. We must, in a richness comparable to what we have done in the arts, have available the tools of many disciplines: rulers, scales, magnets, microscopes, magnifying glasses, telescopes, binoculars, globes, maps, ropes and block and tackle, levers, typewriters . . . .

Children's tools must be good tools. Children need small hammers, for example, and small saws, small pliers and wrenches and screw drivers — *small,* but not toy tools. We have wisely recognized the need for quality instruments in music. Wise teachers insist on pianos of the finest tone, even though young children bang on the piano at times. They insist on good drums and rhythm instruments, on phonographs that produce music and not noise. Young children need similar bona fide quality tools that do well the job they are supposed to do in every area.

A teacher must be a persnickety picker-and-chooser. Everything that goes into her room has to meet her precise standards. No picture goes up on the wall simply because it is "cute" or "pretty" or just to fill up space. Each picture says something and says it well. No book goes on the bookshelf simply because it is available or cheap. Books are carefully chosen for their relevance to her children, for their artistry, for their style. No phonograph record is bought simply because it makes noise. A teacher wants music of the highest quality for her youngsters, music most capable of striking a responsive chord within them. A careful teacher is jealous of the walls in her classroom, the floor, the ceilings, the space — only the very best in her toughest critical judgment gains entrance to them.

A teacher must be a scavenger. Much material for both stimulus and response cannot be bought, even when money is available. Teachers have to engage in a never-ending treasure hunt. The richness of children's learning depends greatly on a teacher's boldness in scrounging for clothing for the dress-up corner; cork and bottle caps and toothpicks, wood shavings and plastics, acorns, pebbles and shells for collage; thread spools and typewriter spools; a wooden barrel, a discarded adding machine, a log . . . .

A teacher must be a community planning engineer. Many activities all go on at once in the young child's classroom. Each activity must have the particular working conditions — room or privacy — that its nature demands. Blocks need ample floor space. Books, puzzles, games need protected areas. Dramatic play calls for isolated space so children can lose themselves in their dream world. Painting must be near water. Good space utilization means good use of materials; it cuts down on traffic accidents as the youngsters move about; it means less crowding and therefore fewer conflicts; it means fewer interruptions and therefore less distraction.

A teacher must be a safety engineer. Climbing apparatus must be tested before children use it, to be sure it is steady and firmly rooted and strong. All wooden surfaces — blocks, boards and boxes, outdoor equipment — must be splinter-free. Nothing can be so weak that it will break under a child's weight: ropes, climbing boards, the surfaces of play houses . . . . A teacher must guard vigilantly against jagged edges, against surfaces that will make children fall, against lures that will lead them in the path of swings or other moving objects.

A teacher must be a maintenance specialist. All materials have to be in tip-top shape for maximum use. Blocks cannot be jumbled; they must be stored by size so that their arrangement encourages children to use them freely yet thoughtfully. Tricycle pedals and handles and seats must be firm so that children are both safe and comfortable. The salvage material at the workbench must be carefully selected: wood soft enough for children to hammer into successfully, nail heads large enough for children to hit. Sand must be the right consistency: soft and powdery if it is to be poured, damp enough if it is to be packed. Paint colors must be clear and full-bodied, not wishy-washy-watery. Clay must be moist and workable.

A teacher must be a cautious, thoughtful manager. She has to decide what materials to put out and what to save. She has to think of yesterday, of today, and of tomorrow. Her goal is stimulation, not over-excitement; enough materials must be available for challenge but not so much as to create confusion. She must seek balance in her materials so the children are stimulated socially, emotionally, physically, and intellectually.

More Stimulus Needed

The initial scene-setting for stimulus leads a teacher into many roles. Each must be played thoughtfully, with self-conscious awareness. At this stage the teacher is teaching largely through materials. Making her materials available in the most telling way is not an offhand job, one she can rush through in the last minute before the children arrive. She must exercise the same precision and calculating decision-making that the most gifted author or lecturer practices in deliberately choosing his very best words.

As the children react to the initial stimulus, the teacher circulates among them. Now she must be a keen observer, assessing whether or not the scene is well set. Is it retaining its yeasty power? For everyone?

Often no major changes are needed for quite a while. The basic equipment of under-six education does not lose its charge quickly. Even five-year-olds who have been to school for two previous years find new possibilities in sand and blocks and wood and clay and paint and boards and boxes — and other children to use them with — for long stretches of time.

Small changes may be called for, however, and can mean the difference between stimulation and monotony for individual children. Sometimes the needed new charge can be provided simply by adding similar pieces of equipment: new books for children to browse through; new records for them to play; more difficult puzzles; more clothing in the dress-up corner; new colors of paint at the easels; a new doll; a different kind of clay; bigger pieces of wood at the workbench; different materials for collage at the work-tables; a new car or boat or truck brought out of reserve.

Sometimes the needed added stimulation can come by placing the same basic equipment in a new area or in a new relationship. The trucks and autos and boats and small figures of people and animals may be moved closer to the block area. Walking boards may be placed between pieces of climbing apparatus or placed at new heights or at new angles. A tricycle and a wagon may be roped together to lead into more complicated play. Paper for the easels may be cut in new and different shapes: ovals, squares, long rectangles, triangles, many-sided and odd-shaped pieces. Newspaper, instead of unprinted paper, may be hung as easel paper, or the unprinted paper may be colored instead of white. The teacher may even start a block construction before the children arrive in the morning. Her small beginning calls attention to the blocks and gives the youngsters a lead to build on.

New Stimulus Needed

At some point major, new stimulus will be needed. Only the teacher observing her children can tell when. She senses that more youngsters seem at loose ends. Their activity lasts a shorter time. Their products — their painting or block building or make-believe or woodwork or clay — seem less innovative.

The time for a change comes sooner with children who have had previous group experience than with those who are meeting group life for the first time. It may come sooner with older children; or when children have had some of the school's materials at home. The challenge of the basic room — its equipment and the presence of co-workers — is very great but: In and of itself it does not last forever.

People who are eager for play to stop, those who want children to sit down, those who think learning is listening, those overly aware that first grade is coming read the signs to mean: Now for the workbooks! Now for the drill! They are impatient with the laboratory way of learning. They leap to the conclusion: Enough of experiences — now is the time to concentrate on "formal teaching." Nothing could be more off-base.

Adults who are very aware of how much some young children know today sometimes lean in this direction, too. Somehow they are led to think that formal sitting-down lessons are the only way of teaching smart young children. They forget how these informed youngsters got that way. It wasn't through formal workbooks. It wasn't through specific exercises and drills. These lucky children had the chance at home for more firsthand experiences. Their parents took them places, their parents did things with them. These smarter boys and girls need still more varied experiences now, just as do the many other youngsters in their group.

The workbook publishers are still another group who hope that the "time for a change" means a change to all-group, sitting-down, formal lessons. Until recently, early education was so small a field that it was hardly worth the notice of publishers. Today the growth of public kindergartens and the spread of Head Start mean that five-year-olds, in particular, are "big business" — a bright new market has opened up. Almost every publisher is exploring ways of using his resources — paper and ink and the printing press — to reach these children.

There *is* one way, the historic way, in which publishers can serve young children: They can publish bona fide books. They can publish honest-to-goodness books, written by creative authors and illustrated by creative artists, books with something informative and provocative to say to the reader or listener.

The trouble is: This is seldom the royal road to riches. Workbooks, exercise books, paper-and-pencil riddle and drill books are where the big money is in early education.

The bombardment of these materials on the schools is so great today that teachers have to learn to say to the bookmen: "Lay off."

The workbooks and exercise books and paper-and-pencil riddle and drill books simply do not fit the age.

These are not sitting-down children. These are not quiet children. They are not meant to be taught all at once in a group, not 20-25 at once, not even 6 or 8 together. At this age such mass instruction only breeds inattention and creates discipline problems.

This is the wrong age for the heavy emphasis on right and wrong, win and lose, on following the rules of the other fellow's game. Five-year-olds almost never seek out this kind of experience for themselves on their own — it has to be imposed on them.

This is the wrong age to expose to command after command: "Draw a line . . . Make a circle . . . Put a mark . . .". Such adult control and domination is appropriate when the learner himself is seeking help. It is inappropriate — it is indecent! — with young children, beginners.

This is the wrong age for stereotyped little line drawings of life. Young children need a richer, fuller diet — they need to deal with life itself.

The workbooks, exercise books, the paper-and-pencil riddle and drill books violate individual differences; they spoil teacher-child relationships; they negate significant developmental characteristics of the children; they distort the flow of a program. Their content is dull, their methods are inappropriate, their goals can be achieved at much less expense in money and with much fuller returns in learning.

A school might wisely buy *one* workbook, exercise book or paper-and-pencil riddle and game book, but never one for every child. The one book could be put on the open shelves, along with all the other materials from which children choose. On rare occasions, usually only momentarily, an individual youngster may seek out the material and be eager to work on it, either on his own or with a teacher's help. Under these special conditions all the vices of the material are minimized, and the strengths they have are maximized.

A school might wisely even buy two, one for this occasional child and one for the teacher's own use, never to use in class but to read at home in bed. The methods are off-base, but the goals of each of the exercises can be a good reminder of what an early education teacher has to be aware of as she involves children in broader, sounder, more stimulating real-life experiences.

Happenings

The children may have outgrown the initial stimulus of the basic equipment, but they have not outgrown their age. They are still young children — albeit a month or two or three older than they were at the start of school. They still learn best through experiences. It *is* time for a change, but the change need not take anything away. All the old basic equipment, indoors and out, is still needed but new events, new Happenings, must be fed in. It is time for more "lectures" and for more "books in the bibliography" — for more stimulus — but in three-year-old, four-year-old, five-year old style. Children need more real-life action so there can be more and better response.

The *field trip* is clearly the best way of providing this added stimulus. Young children cannot read but they can see. They cannot read but they can touch and hear and smell. They cannot read but they can ask questions. A field experience is the prize stimulus for learning for any age: for adults, for graduate students, for college students . . . . We can almost thank God for the young child's illiteracy. It forces us to do the very best thing, to take him to firsthand sources.

Young children's field experiences are short trips, not exhausting journeys. There are good possibilities which should not be overlooked within the school itself, or on the school grounds, or within the close-in immediate neighborhood of the school. Their trips ought not to be to sites teeming with mobs and crowds and masses; these are simple trips, not overexciting and fatiguing.

Most of all, a good trip allows children to be active participants — not mere onlookers or a captive audience for a lecture by a guide. This criterion is of prime importance.

A trip to an airport where youngsters only can look at planes in the distance from a viewing balcony is not as good as a trip which allows the children to get into a plane, sit in the cockpit, talk to the pilot, listen to the intercom, perhaps taxi in the plane along the landing strip . . . . A trip to a farm where the child can only see a cow from behind a fence is not as good as a trip which allows the children to pat the cow, smell the cow, feel the cow's heat, try to milk her . . . . A trip to a supermarket where the children can only walk up and down the aisles is unsatisfactory. The youngsters need to get into the refrigerator room to feel its cold, to climb into the delivery truck to know its hugeness. They need to stamp prices on canned goods, to use the scales, to ring up their purchase on the cash register with the cashier's permission and guidance. A good trip will be short but packed with direct, personal impact.

The longest part of the trip will be the hours the teacher spends getting ready for it. A good trip is never an offhand excursion and seldom a last-minute inspiration. It requires much detailed planning. Careful arrangements have to be made ahead of time to guard against "experts" at the site lecturing at the children — adults love to talk! Arrangements have to be made so that children have the maximum opportunity to touch and to handle and to use. Real dangers must be spotted but imaginary dangers must not be allowed to hold the children back. The teacher needs to make a dry run of the trip to test out its length; children should be stimulated, not exhausted. And the teacher herself must learn ahead of time some of the teaching opportunities that can arise.

Visitors coming into the classroom from the world outside — if the children cannot go out to them — serve the same purpose of stimulation and with almost, not quite, the same intensity. And the same criterion applies to visitors as to trips. The visitor cannot simply be a talker or a distant performer on a stage putting on a demonstration. The children cannot be a sitting audience — they must be in on the act.

When the fireman visits he comes complete with his truck. The children climb on it, they turn on the siren, they clang the bell, perhaps they help hold the nozzle while water streams through the hose. The fireman is in uniform. The children try on his hat, they wear his badge, they try to fill his boots. The visiting policeman comes in his squad car. The children turn on the searchlight and hear the two-way radio. They can touch and use the policeman's handcuffs, his billy club, his whistle, his pad and pencil, and his cap and badge. The reason for bringing in a visiting fireman (or whoever the visitor may be) is not for the children to see him; it is so that they can *be* him.

The occasion of either trip or visitor means that the teacher must now make additions to her room equipment. The dramatic play corner, for example, need not stay a housekeeping corner for all eternity. Children who have been to the supermarket ought to find back in their room the props that will reenforce their trip experience and open up relevant opportunities for response. A grocery cart, a telephone, a cash register, a scale, paper bags, a stamp for marking prices, pads of paper and pencils, white aprons — these are all needed now, just as stoves and refrigerators were timely when children were reacting to their home living.

The outdoor playground of youngsters who have been to a firehouse should now have garden hose and ladders, a siren and bells for tricycles and wagons, and the dress-up clothes — boots, raincoats, helmets, badges — that will help the children recreate their visit more richly in their minds. The teacher must make available whatever closely relates to the children's most recent experience: steering wheels or stethoscopes, tickets or toy money, nurses' caps or pilots' caps, flashlights or tire pumps . . . .

This is the time, too, for good *pictures* — large blown-up photographs and poster-size art work — that will refresh and deepen children's impressions of people and places they have seen, of jobs they have done. Illiterate children can read pictures. We ought to exploit this as a valuable tool for stirring their memories and for bringing them new, more detailed, gripping information. The trouble is: Pictures that say something — ones not merely bland or "cute," not dull, not dead — are very hard to find. Teachers who seek mind-stretching experiences for their youngsters have to pester the public relations offices of industries and businesses, the trade associations, travel agencies, newspaper offices. It takes a lot of hard work to build up a lively picture file and to have on hand the right pictures to cap some stirring firsthand experience.

The *books* a teacher makes available for browsing and those she reads to children can also strengthen the live experiences youngsters have had. Not all stories — or pictures either, for that matter — need tie back to trips and visitors. Many a story stands on its own feet, a new adventure and a new challenge in and of itself. But good teachers are alert to the possibility of using the words and illustrations of a story — the symbols — to carry children back to their Happenings, to carry them more deeply into those Happenings.

Theoretically *movies* could also be a very effective reenforcer of the stimulus youngsters have gotten from their real-life adventures. Now and again a commercially produced film comes close enough to the actual experience children have had to serve this purpose. This is rare, however. The best films for classes of young children usually are amateur films, parent-made or teacher-made, taken of the children on their trips or as visitors have come to them. Slides and displays of still photographs of this same home-grown kind are probably more within the realm of possibility for most groups. These can all offer a good chance for youngsters to see again, to see more slowly, to stop and talk about a Happening in which the youngsters have shared.

Educational TV may also some day reach a point where it can be a true stimulant and a more sound reenforcer. If local stations could ever reduce the cost of mobile camera units so TV could get out into the local community to reproduce the details of local life, it could be a great service to young children. Educational TV, studio-bound, is more of a sedative than a stimulant. Too often it is tied to doing on the screen what the teacher should not do in the classroom: talk at the children and give them artificial lessons.

None of these back-up experiences — pictures, stories, movies, slides, photos — need be all-group experiences. The "organized" quality of the usual all-group Show-and-Tell session has set a bad standard that ought to be dropped. It is beautifully designed to let one person talk, to let one person feel involved, while all the others wiggle or doze or let their minds wander. Young children need the fullest sense of being "in" on what is going on. The larger the group the smaller the likelihood that children will care. They will be present but unmoved. Stimulus is strongest when it touches each person. We ought always to strive for the small setting — the subgroup of a teacher with three or four children, the private group of the teacher with one child alone — as much as possible.

None of these back-up experiences, especially not story time, should be used to keep children quiet. The aim is to stir them up. A story is not a tranquilizer before lunch or before going out of doors or before going home. It is a springboard for interruptions, for questions, for comments, for freeing the train of thought that the story starts.

Many *activities* are possible right within the classroom or on the room's play yard which also serve well to carry children's thinking into new areas. These "at-home" Happenings, like everything else, are usually at their best in smaller subgroups. Then everyone has the chance to take part. Cooking is one good example. Four or five or six youngsters and the teacher may make a gelatin dessert or a pudding or cookies or pancakes or a stew or applesauce .... But there are no end of possibilities: Four or five may dig a garden spot and plant seeds out-of-doors; four or five may dig up some garden soil for an indoor bulb or seed planting; a few youngsters may work with the teacher in setting up a terrarium or building a pet cage or painting a playhouse or setting eggs in the incubator to hatch.

Exhibits are another way of bringing stimulation into the home base. A good classroom ought to be a lively museum — you never know what you will see! Today's exhibit may be a snake, a mouse, baby ducks, a kitten or a bird, pollywogs or minnows — it may even be a human baby. The exhibit may be a bird's nest, antlers, a musical instrument, a ship's bell. Teachers, with the help of parents and others, can reach far out into a community that children cannot get to and bring that community right to the children's doorstep. A classroom "museum" can be like the very best of our public museums, not a "hands-off" place where you simply stare but one which invites you to handle and touch.

Writing in the Classroom

The teacher's continuous use of the *written word* is one of the most important stimuli she provides. The written word is the universal tool of all the disciplines. Every subject matter field has its recorded information. Observations are written down. Notes are kept. Records are filed. Words are bound into books. Yesterday's word — in file or notebook or printed book — is checked. This tool, the written word, must be used abundantly in our classrooms for young children.

Youngsters — even three-year-olds to some extent but especially four and five-year-olds — must see adults writing. They must see us reading. They must see us continually using paper and pencil, paper and pen, paper and typewriter, paper and print. When the children are cooking, the recipe should be written out on easel paper in manuscript. When the children go on a trip, the notice should be posted on the door: *The Fours have gone to the zoo.*

Simple announcements and plans should be written out on the chalkboard or on the easel: *The nurse is coming today.* Notes of reminders should be written: *We need 15 cartons of milk ... We need more red paint.* Permission letters — "May the Fives visit the fire boat?" — and thank-you letters — "Thank you for letting the Fives visit the fire boat" — should all be written. The teacher should seize every reasonable opportunity to write out everything: letters, records, labels, directions.... The standard ought to be: Don't just say it, and don't just keep it in your mind — tell it to the world in writing, too.

One rule ought to be absolutely clear, however: The teacher should do as much writing as appropriate *but no child should have to read it.* That step is up to each youngster. A few will read every word — they will gobble up every piece of writing around. Some occasionally will show interest and will ask for help in figuring out words. Very many won't even be aware that the writing is in the room, any more than they notice a smudge on the window. And the writing should not interfere with their life any more than the smudge on the window does. The writing must be available, just as easels are, but no child need have his nose rubbed in it any more than he has to paint simply because the easels are available.

The Sequence of Learning: Where To Begin?

Which new added stimulus should be chosen first? Where should a teacher begin? The answer that seems to make the greatest sense is: *Begin wherever the liveliest action is.*

No trip is so precious that young children everywhere must take it first. No one visitor must always be the first to every classroom. No activity is so foundational that all others depend on it. Nor is it crucial that certain facts or skills or concepts be mastered first.

Only one thing really matters: A teacher must stay close to the cutting edge of children's enthusiasms. She must choose significant Happenings, rich in potential learnings — this is not amusement or busy work. But a teacher must have the freedom to seize upon the most gripping event available to her group.

This policy of maximum leeway for a teacher to plan with the interests of her particular group foremost in her mind is contrary to common practice with older children. The prevailing approach — one many kindergartens follow, too — is to have a course of study for a year or a sequence of units for a semester: Our Community Helpers, The Home, The Farm.... It is contrary to the recommendations of some scholars, newly interested in the problems of child education, who tend to believe that their particular field must be mastered in a step-by-step orderly progression.

The adult logic behind a planned sequence of units looks fine on paper. In practice, too often it conflicts with the young child's psycho-*logic* make-up. These are children with unpredictable attention spans. The fixed units become binding in the classroom. They often force teachers to try to hold youngsters to activities long after their interest has flagged. They make teachers ignore gripping events that unpredictably capture children's concern or ignore the unusual teaching opportunities that come along unexpectedly: the steam shovel digging at the corner, a house being moved down the street, a bird building a nest outside the window.

These are egocentric children. The Happening has to touch *them*. This personal involvement is the key to their motivation, the key to holding their attention, the key to their caring. Units planned in advance, units planned for children in general, can leave them cold; Happenings right at their doorstep can stir them up.

These are beginners. They are making their initial investigations and discoveries in many areas. At a later age they can put what they have learned in some logical order in their minds. Now there are significant learnings wherever they turn, and their high interest is more important than the logical order. A trip to the bakery or a ride in a truck, the visit of a mother and her baby to class, the experience of cooking a stew or establishing a terrarium — all can open up new, provocative trains of thought to these children. They are new to this world, not old hands who have been everywhere and done everything.

The temptation of school systems to write out a kindergarten or Head Start course of study is very great, but we ought to resist the temptation. A much better use of teachers' time is the development of a comprehensive list of the many significant Happenings available to a particular school, an all-inclusive detailing of the resources for trips and visitors and activities. A teacher can then wisely choose from such an extensive list the stimulus most

needed by her group at the time. Energy would also be well spent
elaborating the possible developments stemming from one (or two
or three) of these Happenings, spelling out the varied teaching
opportunities that might emerge from one experience. Such a prototype could serve as a guide and useful eye-opener as to how all
other Happenings might be exploited. The prototype would be a
sample, a taste. Like the list of Happenings it should not at all
be intended to tie a teacher's hands. The right place to begin and
the right steps to take next cannot come from paper. They have
to come from the teacher's assessment of her children. For any
one teacher the right place to start is with whatever significant
Happenings will stir up her children the most.

RESPONSE

Once the teacher has set the stimulation in motion — whether
through the initial equipment of the classroom, through altera-
tions of it, through trips or visitors or through classroom activities
— the next step is the children's response. The youngsters go to
work. The teacher stands back a bit.

Play Time and Work Time

The day may begin indoors or out. Time and weather are key
factors. The day care center, because of its early hours, will probably usually start indoors. But wherever the day begins, the greatest gift the teacher can bring to the children at this point in the
instructional process is freedom. The children are free to choose
what they will do. They are free to use the material in whatever
way seems important to them. They are free to stay with the material as long as they choose and free to work with whomever
they choose. Through setting the scene for stimulation, the teacher
has done her initial teaching. Very soon she will have more teaching to do in other ways. But right now, starting the very minute
they arrive, the children need the chance to go to work on their
own, to get involved in their own learning.

Words to describe clearly this important part of the young
child's day are hard to find. At the college level you would prob-

ably call this "discussion time" or time for "committee work" or for "buzz sessions" or maybe even for "bull sessions." At upper grade and high school levels this would be the time for themes and reports; the students organize all that has been coming in to them and try to make some of it their own. At the under-six level this period is most commonly called "play time," sometimes "free play."

This name applies to the overwhelmingly largest part of the young child's day in school. The teacher-instigated stimulus periods — trips, visitors, real-life classroom activities — are not play times. Juice, toileting, story time, music are not play times. But play does fill most of the important blocks of time on most days. The children play for thirty or forty minutes or so, indoors or out, at the start. As their energy runs down the teacher changes the pace briefly — probably with toileting, snack, story, or music. And then play or free play begins again, outdoors if the group started inside, indoors if the day began in the outdoor classroom.

In the day care center the same basic sequence continues on. Lunch and sleep form the next transition — these are not play times. Nor are the waking and toileting and dressing and snack times. After that the children customarily go outdoors to play and then come indoors to play, or vice versa. The one exception occurs as the day nears its very end. If the children are tired from their long spell of group living or if they become anxious as the time for the arrival of the long-separated mother draws near, the teacher may have to inject herself in a more central position — perhaps as a storyteller — to become a stabilizing force.

Those unfortunate schools that have no outdoor classroom of their own basically follow this same sequence too, but they cannot change location. The children play — there is a break — and then children play again with different materials available, all indoors. The absence of an outdoor classroom can put pressure on a teacher to fill the time with more teacher-organized and all-group activities than young children need: organized games, assemblies of the class, workbooks. But a wise teacher resists the pressure. If her original stimulus has played itself out, she seeks more sound Happenings rather than busy-work so that her children can have a springboard into more sound play.

Play sounds wicked as a central activity of a school. Free play sounds worse. But young children's play is not light-hearted activity. Least of all is it wild, running-screaming activity. Play is a time for deep concentration. Children become completely absorbed in blocks or make-believe or paints or in building at the workbench. Play is a time of earnestness and intensity. The instant a teacher senses a lackadaisical quality, a random or scattered quality, she knows something is wrong. Either energy is at a low ebb, or the stimulus has run down, or the setting is wrong, or something — it is time for a change. Children at play are like men at work they love; like students at study that enthralls them; like artists in the act of creation.

Play for young children is not recreation activity, not recess activity. It is not leisure-time activity nor escape activity. Free play is thinking time for young children. It is language time. Problem-solving time. It is memory time, planning time, investigating time. It is organization-of-ideas time, when the young child uses his mind and body and his social skills and all his powers in response to the stimuli he has met.

"Independent work" could be the label for this activity. Many schools call this "work time," not "play time." It is that. The instant a teacher senses a let-down, pointless repetition — anything less than hard work — she knows something is wrong. It is time for a change.

Free play is "free" because the child chooses: what he does, how he does it, how long he does it, with whom he does it. Free play is "play" because the activity strikes so deep a chord of pleasure within the child. But free play is learning. When the learning stops, something is wrong. It is time for a change.

The Talking Teacher

In free play the children are learning through their use of materials. They are learning from each other. They are learning from their very busy, continuous, internal process of puzzling, wondering, and organizing their thoughts and impressions. These are sometimes spoken of as "incidental learnings." The term is not one that minimizes these learnings. The children's drive to play makes some of these learnings the most acceptable, most retained learnings of all. "Incidental" suggests only the unpredictable content of the learnings. Active playing-working children can cover the waterfront in their verbal and physical explorations.

But while the children freely play, they learn from the teacher too. The teacher is not passive — free-play time is a very busy time for her. Play time is a time for "incidental learnings." It is also the time for highly pinpointed instruction.

The teacher circulates from group to group, from individual to individual. She stays close to the children. Children's play time is the time for the teacher to use her knowledge of subject matter. To do this well she has to hear what is on children's lips, read what is on their faces, sense what is in their minds. She is constantly seeking for every teaching opportunity that can arise out of the youngsters' activity.

The teacher of young children needs a lot of information at her fingertips. Each of the fields of learning has its own body of facts; each its broad concepts which emerge from those facts; each its own terminology, the correct words and the technical words that scholars use for the phenomena in their field of study. When a teacher has planned a Happening in advance — a trip to the filling station, a train ride, cutting out the pumpkin and baking the pie — she can anticipate better some of the queries that may come and some of the opportunities she may have to take the lead in making points. She has to spend a lot of time organizing herself: What are the key facts involved in this activity? What are the big ideas and important generalizations that can emerge? But children at play ask countless unexpected questions. A teacher has to be a source of information, not misinformation. She has to be able to pass on accurate facts, not myths or old wives' tales.

A teacher needs more information than she can carry around. She must have access to resources to supplement her own store of knowledge. A good encyclopedia and a good dictionary should be available in the room for the teacher, as commonplace a resource for her as easels and books and dolls and blocks are for the children. Other source books are needed, too: reference books in special fields, adult books that deal with the areas in which the children are involved — Bird Life, Engines, Mammals . . . . Standard operating procedure should be for the teacher to say many times a day: "I don't know. Let's look it up." Or: "I think I am right. Let's double-check to be sure."

The resources need not always be a book. The teacher should also have access to specialists whom she can consult in person and by telephone. It is important for children to be a part of this whole process of uncovering new information and of checking information with firsthand and secondary sources.

To build sound information, good language, and valid generalizations, the teacher is ever alert for the chance to say the right words to the right person at the right time. It is all too easy to talk too much *at* children. Talking creates the illusion of teaching but the wise teacher knows: There is little learning unless someone is listening and unless he cares.

Some teachers cannot resist the temptation to be center-stage. They cannot resist the temptation to overuse flannel boards — a chance to talk and play the role of actress-magician! Such teachers love Planning Times when all the children come together at the start of the day to confess what they expect to do and to receive the teacher's blessing. They have badly-named "Work Times" when the teacher does all the work, asking questions, prompting answers . . . and maintaining order.

To be sure, other teachers of young children talk too little. They participate too little. Once they have set the stage for stimulus — they often do this too little, too — they become mere bystanders. They want the children to be active, they want them to be free. But they have not found the way of playing a constructive role themselves while the youngsters are constructively engaged.

A wise teacher knows she can always safely and constructively speak "welcome words," words a child will be glad to hear. She recognizes when she has to speak less welcome words and is skilled in saying them so they have the best chance of sinking in. But she can keep quiet, too, if talking would make her an unneeded intruder.

Welcome Words

Praise for what a child has done is always welcome. The teacher gives support, every chance she gets, to the qualities she wants to build into children: curiosity, creativity, independence, generosity, thoughtfulness....

Communication that firms up what a child has said is always welcome. "You're right. That is a pyramid"... "That cloud is a thunderhead. How did you know that?"... "You *do* have nine blocks. Let's count them together: One, two, three...."

Answers to the questions a child voices are welcome communication. The youngster listens to the response because he thought up the question. "Water freezes when the temperature drops to 32 degrees. Let's get the thermometer and I'll show you where 32 degrees is."

A teacher close to children can volunteer the answer to the unspoken question on the tip of a child's tongue or in the back of his mind. She does not always have to wait for the words to come out. Or she can ask the leading question, a slight step ahead of where the child is in his thinking: "What could you do with that?" ... "Does that remind you of anything you have at home?"... "What do you call something that feels like that?"

The teacher plays this same welcome role when she makes signs to go on children's block-building: *Airport ... Ticket Office ....* She is in tune with what is on a child's mind when she enriches his tricycle play with an appropriate sign: *Stop ... Slow ... Gas ... No Parking.* Or when, indoors or out, she helps him elaborate his dramatic play: *Quiet. Hospital ... Tires For Sale ... Men At Work.*

The active, circulating, listening teacher speaks welcome words when she gives a child the help he needs when he needs it. She may speak words of general encouragement — "You're getting it. Keep trying!" — if they are enough to spur a child on. She may speak words of specific advice, if a child needs this kind of help: "Try lifting one end first"... "That pole is too short, isn't it? I know where we have a longer pole that you can use."

Less Welcome Words

All teachers, of course, speak many less welcome words in the course of every day. Often the words are unnecessary and wasted. A child gives some lead — a question, a puzzled look — and we start in with welcome words but we don't know when to stop. We are so eager to teach that we fail to teach. We tell the child much more than he wants to know. A wise teacher never overstays her welcome. She stands ready to exit gracefully when a child's interest flags.

Some of our less welcome words have to be said, however. They are words of prohibition, words of correction that the child has not asked for. But the words are necessary to keep him from hurting himself or others, from damaging property or from persisting in some error. Under-six or thirty-six, words of prohibition and of correction are hard words for any of us to take. A teacher does not back away from saying them when she has to. If she is wise, however, she searches for the way of saying them that will make them as palatable as possible to the child. She wants these less welcome words to sink in. She has no stake in having them shrugged off because the child finds them too unpleasant.

The less welcome words should not be wishy-washy. They should not sound like a suggestion when they are meant to be a command; they should not sound like a question when they are meant to be a statement; they should not sound like a choice when there is no choice, when the child is expected to do what the teacher is saying. Wishy-washy words only add to a child's confusion and almost always lead to more trouble.

The less welcome words should be firm but they should not be angry words. A youngster may have behaved badly or he may have made some irritating error. But if the teacher jumps all over him he has to defend himself. We all react in the same fashion — our egos are important to all of us. When the words sound like an attack on the person, the lesson gets lost. The child becomes so busy defending himself against the anger, so busy with conflicting emotions, that he cannot think straight. And straight thinking, after all, ought to be the goal of all of our words, the welcome and the less welcome ones.

The less welcome words should not be broadcast. When they must be said they ought to be eyeball-to-eyeball, private conversation. Young children have to save face, we all do. The public reprimand, the public correction put even a young child on the hot spot. His thoughts go into how to escape, not into how to learn to improve and do better the next time.

The less welcome words should not be nagging words. If a teacher has to say the same thing, day after day, a hundred times, she gets no medal for doing her duty assiduously. The chances are that she is wasting her time, merely going through the motions of teaching. The child obviously has tuned her out — the words are not getting over. Whenever she finds herself nagging, the wise teacher reassesses what is going on. More talking — even louder, tougher talking — probably is not the way to reach the youngster at this time.

A better approach may lie in backing up the words with action. We may have to stand by a child so that our presence helps him act better. We may have to take his hand or take his arm — as a friend, not an arresting policeman — to give extra support to what we say.

Or a better approach may lie in making some change in the classroom environment: rearranging the equipment, removing some troublesome material, changing the time schedule. Settings can say "No" for us — or "Yes" — in an impersonal way that often can be more effective than any spoken word.

There are times, too — much as we might wish otherwise — when our best bet is to bite our tongue and bide our time. The smart approach for the moment may be to do nothing.

We usually can afford to play this waiting game when only language is at stake, when the trouble is what a child *says* rather than what he does. One example is the problem of changing Head Start children's language of the street to the language of the school, both their linguistic peculiarities and their more colorful expressions. The children's words may offend us but the world won't end because of any words they use. In language — in many other areas, too — young children have to make "mistakes" first, a whole batch of them, before they are ready to change. Words that are so unwelcome today that they bounce off the child become welcome words in some tomorrow when the child himself begins to see a reason for changing.

Silent Teaching

Some of the best teaching any of us ever does occurs when we don't say a word. We are not telling anyone anything. We are not showing them anything. We don't even know we are teaching but the children have their eyes on us, often very consciously. They don't even know they are learning, but they lap up our behavior.

This process of silent teaching is called *Identification*. Children feel with us, they like us, and they want to be like us. Identification is one of the most potent educative forces, and it operates at all age levels. In homes the well-loved parents of young children are style-setters — they teach more through their love than they ever could through words alone. Elementary youngsters, the high school age, even college students have their adult "heroes" and "heroines." The process of identification goes on, too, among young children. Older brothers and sisters at home, older boys and girls in a class or in a school also serve as models. This is the reason Head Start so strongly urges using junior and senior high school volunteers in its program. Every growing person has his eyes up.

The youngest children, most of all, hitch their wagons to a star.

Their dependence — their smallness, their newness on this earth, their ignorance and impotence — makes them exceptionally open to the lessons that can come through identification. Identification has an unusually valuable place in the good teaching of young children. What a teacher is, what a teacher does, how a teacher acts, form a large part of what a teacher teaches.

There is one joker, however, under-six or over-six: Children identify only with people they like! The rest of us are mere passersby, parts of the scenery, wallflowers. We may set spectacular examples but if the children have no deep feeling for us, we simply are not on their wavelength — we have to reach them some other way. Identification only operates when relationships are close, warm, friendly. Silent teaching is nil when relationships are cold or casual.

The good teacher of young children goes out of her way to build intimate bonds. The prize way for her to do her wooing is to spend time alone with each child. She searches for the intimate touch: visiting a child at his home; having something personal to say as a greeting when he arrives in the morning; giving concentrated help when a youngster is in trouble; working a puzzle or reading a story or taking a short walk with one child alone; holding a youngster's hand or sitting by his side or tousling his hair.

Every youngster has to feel: This is *my* teacher, as if he were the apple of her eye. It is no simple job for a teacher to convey this sense of caring to each and every one. Some lucky youngsters are magnetized — they attract a teacher's warm feelings in no time at all. Often a teacher has to go to extra lengths — arranging private little chats, making personal telephone calls to a child — to reach other youngsters who are less quickly lovable. But often the more quiet children or those who get in our hair are the ones who most need to have a crush on someone they can pattern themselves after.

Once a child is crazy about her, a teacher teaches every second of the time. The child listens better to what she says and — more important — he keeps his eye on what she does. The teacher is on the job when she is talking and knows she is teaching — she is on the job all the time, teaching through everything she does.

The massive learnings that come through identification often are unappreciated. The learnings are so quiet. The learnings only show up later. The learnings are less apt to be specific, the kind that can be measured on a test. But broad attitudes, values, the points of view, the style and approach of a teacher do become part of a child, if he thinks she really is a prize.

A teacher's way of talking becomes a part of him. If our children feel close to us, the language we use is the language we teach.

A teacher's sense of beauty sinks in: The gaiety and color and good taste of her clothing, the attention she gives to the charm of her room, her selective response — on trips and on the play yard — to objects of beauty: a flower, a bird, a cloud, a color.

A teacher's openness to experience is absorbed. Children who love her are aware of her freedom from fear of snakes, mice, bugs; of her enjoyment of snow and cold, of thunder, of the wind; of her relish for new tastes; of the way she reaches out to the different and the unusual.

Everything about a well-loved teacher gets under a child's skin: Her patience. Her humor. Her reasonableness. Her kindness, her helpfulness to those in distress . . . . Walt Whitman spoke of "a child (who) went forth every day and the first object he looked upon, that object he became and that object became part of him for the day, or a certain part of the day, or for many years, or stretching cycles of years." When that object is a well-loved teacher, the child's learnings can be manifold.

THE SCOPE OF THE CURRICULUM

Covering all the fields of learning is a formidable task, not an easy one for any level of education. The traditional elementary school — and kindergarten — approach to a solution to this question of the scope of the curriculum, as with the question of sequence in the curriculum, has been the development of curriculum guides. This approach, however, is not well suited to programs for young children.

Problems of a Balanced Diet

We do better to follow the approach of colleges. The college solution to the problem of a balanced diet is to have "distribution requirements." Colleges try to provide experiences fairly evenly in each of the four broad areas of knowledge: the Humanities, Mathematics and the Sciences, the Social Sciences, Health and Physical Education. Education under six can do the same thing. Periodically, perhaps once a month or so, a teacher can look back over a group's total Happenings and look back over each child's involvement in them. Has there been an unnecessary lumping in any one or two broad areas of study? Has there been a reasonable balance among all four? This periodic checkup can tip us off as to whether we need to strive more energetically to open up experiences in some new directions.

The goal cannot be, nor need it be, an even- steven approach — equal time for every field of study. For one thing, *the age of the children* means that some fields must be treated very lightly now to receive greater emphasis later. In general, the younger the child the less apt he is to be excited about or to truly understand the faraway in either time or distance. The younger the child the less apt he is to become concerned about the inert and the immobile. Three, four, and five-year-olds are more likely to respond to what they can see and touch and use. They are more apt to become involved in whatever crosses their path in some noisy, active, functional fashion. A fossil may intrigue some few young children — the chances are slight that it will excite many. The Washington Monument — tall, statuesque, dead — is more apt to become a center for running up and down the steps than for any meaningful lessons in history or art or community planning.

A school's location also makes complete, balanced, A through Z coverage difficult and undesirable. An urban school may have an occasional chance to teach geology when an excavation is being dug. All schools for young children inevitably have few chances to teach astronomy. Inland schools, seacoast schools, suburban schools, warm-weather schools, all schools have special opportunities — and limitations. No school has all the resources close at hand to promote the utmost of what children could learn if a specific location and setting confronted the children with a challenge.

A teacher's own background is a third obstacle to a curriculum of perfect balance and complete coverage. Colleges face up to this fact: "We have a very strong physics department" . . . "Our work in psychology is rather weak." But colleges are lucky. They can subdivide human knowledge and parcel out the specialties. The teacher of young children is the whole faculty, all by herself. She is the physicist and psychologist and philosopher and artist and musician and mathematician . . . the A-ist through Z-ist. And no one can be good at everything.

A teacher's enthusiasm is the secret ingredient in all good teaching — it must not be lost. A teacher has to be excited about what she and her youngsters are doing. Teaching cannot be her duty — it has to be her love. You can count any child lucky whose teacher is a little "unbalanced," head-over-heals in love with activities that involve mathematics or science or art or literature . . . . The curriculum may be somewhat uneven but the chances are that the children are in a good class.

A need does exist to guard against avoidable imbalance, that which occurs through inadvertence or bad planning or from blindly following tradition. One way of doing this is to check a classroom diary periodically against the framework of the liberal arts. Then, if need be, we can always set out aggressively to correct any imbalances and to fill in any important gaps.

The Common Strands in Subject Matter

Another safeguard for insuring adequate coverage and a balanced curriculum is for the teacher to be aware of some of the pervasive themes that permeate all the fields of study, and to take every opportunity to drive them home.

The subject-matter labels make the disciplines sound so separate and specialized. Yet there are broad strands which ignore the labels and jump the fences. These concerns are a part of each and every field. A teacher who keeps these across-the-board themes in mind can teach simultaneously in more than one field at once. Whenever she hits at one of these themes she teaches many subject matters, no matter how the label might read on the activity in which the children are engaged.

All scholars hold one overall view which can be stated like this: *Man lives in a universe of mystery in which there is order and continuity and interrelationship.* Broadly speaking, this is the stance of the ichthyologist at his particular site of operation, the stance of the geologist at his; this is the set of the psychologist as he studies individuals, and it is the attitude of the sociologist as he examines groups; the archeologist studies the past, the political scientist is more involved in today, but both hold this outlook. Each and every one — and biologists and nutritionists, geographers, philosophers, A through Z — is trying to unravel the mystery by finding some part of the inherent order and continuity and interrelationship in order to give man more control over the universe.

This one broad, shared viewpoint leads to other common attitudes and approaches. Some of these attitudes are felt more keenly by specialists in mathematics and in the social and natural sciences; some more keenly by workers in the humanities. But there is overlap and interplay. When the classroom rings with common themes it makes little difference whether the children are cooking applesauce or digging a trench, visiting a fireboat or planting a garden. They are working in no one subject matter — they are in all of them.

Regardless of his label or area of specialization — astronomer or artist, botanist or author — the adult scholar looks on life around him with a *sense of wonder.* He takes nothing for granted within his own field. Because this is his training, he brings this same sense of wonder to all of life. Nothing passes him by. Nothing is too small, too insignificant for his curious notice. Nothing is ordinary. The scholar — psychologist, statistician, musician, biologist — is open. His eyes are open, his ears are open, his nostrils are open, his pores are open.

He is aware of and captivated by the phenomena around him. The anthropologist is aware of the way babies are held when they are bathed. The criminologist selectively hears the sternness in a mother's voice. The agronomist stoops to feel the crumbly quality of the soil. The nutritionist tastes the thickness of a pea hull with his tongue. Each specialist has his particular focus but all have an identical response: The world is full of fascinating phenomena.

The young child's world can seem very everydayish to adults. In that world there are few seemingly spectacular incidents. The child's life is made up of the plop of hot cereal, the whistling of the teakettle, the dew on the grass and the frost on the window, red and green paints running together, wood floating in the water table and a metal ring sinking, blocks toppling, the whirr of wind, chocolate melting in the hand, gum that costs five cents . . . . The scholar's sense of wonder transforms a similar, "ordinary" world into the *extra*-ordinary.

A good classroom helps its children look on their small world as a part of a universe of never-ending mystery. We do this when, no matter what Happening the children are involved in, we teach them to stop, look, and listen . . . and feel and taste and smell. We foster a sense of wonder when we give fullest support to the questioning mind: What is it? Where does it come from? What is it made of? What is it for? We do it when we spur close-up examination, through our own example and through the encouragement we give to children. When we work in these ways to build a sense of wonder we move toward a balanced curriculum because this openness, this excited awareness, is a common quality of every discipline.

Regardless of his label or area of specialization the adult scholar approaches all phenomena with a *commitment to evidence*. He wants the facts. He is not content with surface appearances or quick impressions or say-so or hearsay. The scholar is driven by insistent questions: How do you know? How can you tell? How can you be sure? He experiments, so that he can be more clear about what he is seeing. He compares, so that he can be more certain. He digs into the background, to get the full picture. He records all evidence so that there is no forgetting and no mis-understanding. The scholar is a skeptic until all the facts are in. He then becomes a believer only as far as the facts will carry him. The scholar is the detective in this universe of mystery.

A good classroom prods its young children to get evidence. We push them into the detective role whenever we encourage puzzling and wondering: Why does the Jello harden? Why did the blocks fall? What made the aquarium water turn green? Why did the wood split? Why do you think Bobby hit you? We foster the detective role whenever we support experimentation and comparison: "Can you think of another way of doing that?" . . . "Let's try it again to see what happens" . . . "We will look carefully tomorrow to see if it stays the same." We build a commitment to evidence when we take every opportunity to write down facts for children so that they can see a record kept: of their height, of the temperature, the rainfall, the weight of a frog, the number of days the eggs have been in the incubator . . . Whenever we emphasize the need for evidence we cut across every subject-matter line.

Thirdly, regardless of his label or area of specialization the adult scholar is concerned with *classification and grouping.* He tries to relate one observation to another. He searches constantly for the broader meaning. He pushes from the specific to concept, from concept to broader generalization. He searches everlastingly for unity, through time and across-the-board. He is persuaded that there is order, if he can discover it; that there is continuity, if he can discover it; that there are interrelationships.

We help children think along these lines when we lead them into seeing connections: "What does the marshmallow taste like? . . . and what does it feel like, look like, what does it make you think of?" We teach in many fields at once when we introduce children to the search for similarities and differences: "Have you ever tasted anything like this before?" . . . "It's round and soft, almost like a what?" . . . "Do you think it bounces like a ball? Try it and see." We push the subject-matter walls down when we lead children into thinking back to causes, when we prod them into puzzling about future probabilities, and when we help them connect what they are doing to something else they know.

Adult scholars hold a fourth passion in common: Regardless of their label or field of specialization they all see *man as the potential master of the mystery.* They believe man can control his environment. In particular, the artist and the musician, the playwright and architect and author and poet and sculptor, hold this vision. They see man as a creator. But so, too, do the mathematicians and scientists. This is the image when they build our planes, develop our space program, make our weather, control our population, multiply our food and water resources. It is the image of the social scientists as they wrestle with the problems of war and peace, internationally and interpersonally. Man, a creator, is the underlying concept of health workers as they battle disease. All scholars believe that the whole point of getting the facts and comprehending the law and order and interrelationships is so that man can make his universe a better place in which to live.

We build this same spirit — we teach what every discipline wants its students to feel — when we support children's own fresh, innovative ways of responding to their world. We do it when we liven their language: "How else could you say 'quick as a flash'? Quick as a . . . what?" This is not language teaching alone — it teaches the creative spirit that floods the sciences and mathematics and the social sciences. We do it whenever we give special support to a child's originality: "I like the way you painted your picture — it's different from everyone else's." This is not a comment on art alone — it boosts a spirit essential to the sciences and mathematics and the social sciences. We build the sense of man as master when we foster independence, when we spur problem-solving. The particular field does not matter — the spirit cuts across all of them.

EVALUATION

Evaluation is so important that we all ought to be very good at it. The pressing, practical question of retention or promotion, a matter of vital importance to parents and to a child, is involved. Even beyond this, teachers need to know whether or not they are achieving what they set out to do. And if we are ever to end the shortage of programs for young children our country has to know: Do nursery school and kindergarten and day care and Head Start pay off?

Unfortunately, under-six education is not good at evaluation.

Reading Readiness

One reason for this inadequacy is the over-anxiety of parents about reading. We have let reading and reading readiness take

over the whole show. Many kindergartens measure the effective-
ness of their total program by children's scores on reading readiness tests. Retention or promotion is settled almost exclusively
by these scores. All other learnings fade into a pale fourth place.
Until we help people simmer down about reading, until it settles
into its appropriate place of importance, evaluation will be skewed.

Programs will be skewed, too. Understandably, teachers aim at
what will be measured. Reading readiness tests determine much
of the content and many of the methods of kindergarten programs.
If visual discrimination is an item on the test, the safest way of
teaching can seem to be to have the children draw a line, under
supervision, from one picture to another in a workbook. You can't
take a chance on letting them play on their own with blocks or
taking them on a field experience at the post office. These wide-
open approaches seem to have too many variables — the children
may learn things that won't show up on the test. If the ability
to follow a story sequence is an item on the test, the safest way of
teaching can seem to be to have the children draw a line, under
supervision, from one picture to another in a workbook. A teacher
easily comes to feel that she cannot afford to let children develop
their own imaginative story-line as they play on tricycles or on
the jungle gym or at the sandbox. The contrived, controlled lesson
produces results that fit the test better, but such lessons fit
children very badly.

Lessening Anxiety

We can, however, do a lot more than we now do to lessen the
over-anxiety about reading. For one thing, we can be sure that
parents are informed. We can make certain that they know about
all the rich and varied experiences their children are having. Some
of the over-worry about reading boils up because of bad communication. Parents have no way of knowing about the many exciting
Happenings in the group involving science, mathematics, the social
sciences, literature and the humanities. Unaware, operating in a
vacuum, their concerns latch on to reading. To counteract this
teachers must strive aggressively to keep parents abreast of the
many opportunities for solid learnings in their program. The more
we do this, the less reading will seem the be-all and end-all of
group life.

See pages 152-157 for a further discussion of parent participation, Teacher's Newsletters, and other techniques for building parent understanding of a group's program.

We can have a sensible policy on promotion, too. This will help lesson the fixation on reading. That policy ought to be: No retention in kindergarten ... No five-year-old should fail. There might be the very rare exception when for a variety of reasons — never reading readiness alone — a prescription is worked out for a particular child, with the full concurrence of his parents, which includes repeating kindergarten. But certainly the general policy ought to be: Every child moves on. No one should have to achieve a particular reading readiness score in order to be eligible for first grade.

To enter any first grade a youngster just has to be the right age. Schools which have no kindergartens have no entrance requirements for their first grades. There is no reason on the face of the earth why a school which does have a kindergarten should establish hurdles in the way of its first grade entrance. If parents know that their child will move on with his group as a matter of course there is less need than ever to give readiness tests in kindergarten, and less pressure to trim teaching to fit them.

We can use more appropriate readiness "tests," too. Teachers need to know, and parents will always want to know, how their child is doing in reading. The child's behavior is the best answer to that. Behavior is much better than any test score from a contrived, made-up situation. What a child actually does in a classroom which is filled with countless opportunities to read is the best possible key to a child's readiness. Does he notice the signs and labels and writing in the room? Does he ask the teacher to write out words to embellish his dramatic play? Does he want to dictate stories? Does he try to figure out words on his own? Does he turn to books when he has completely free choice? On trips is he aware of street signs and house numbers, of signs in stores and on products, of price markers, of writing on the sides of busses and trucks? Does he choose games that call for matching, and what level of matching seems to be his comfortable *modus operandi*? Or does he pass by all the opportunities to read? Are they ignored by him, never catching his eye?

Readiness is a special mixture of both power and desire. A child's free choice — what captures his interest and holds him persistently; what he rejects and ignores — is the best evidence of where a child stands. When parents know that a teacher is collecting this evidence day after day, not simply on some one "test day" alone, their anxieties diminish somewhat.

In this same vein — perhaps most of all — we must assure parents that we, too, value reading. We must leave no doubt in their minds that we, too, want children to learn to read as quickly as is right for them. We must make it crystal clear that we would not want to hold any child back in his reading skill, any more than we would want to hold him back in the development of any of his capacities. Some of the intense obsession with reading and the eagerness for reading readiness scores comes because parents think school people are fighting them — they want one thing and we want something else.

We feed the flames of this unnecessary conflict when we say: "No. We do not teach reading in kindergarten (or in nursery school or day care or Head Start)." We feed the flames when we reply in "pedagese" that leaves parents unsure and unsettled: "No. We do not teach reading, but we do teach 'reading readiness'." There have been sound reasons for these traditional responses. Teachers have wanted to protect children. They know that so very few youngsters at these early ages are ready to go deeply into reading or to stay with it very long. Teachers haven't wanted to increase the pressure on children, but the weazel words and the negative words have unfortunately promoted just that.

We will do much more to help parents feel at ease if we say: "We *do* teach reading. We work very hard to teach it but — keep in mind — *under-six methods of teaching differ from over-six education.*" This is welcome news for parents *and* it is being fairer to ourselves, for under-six education must teach reading . . . and all the 3 R's . . . and the Liberal Arts. If we are clear on what we are doing, we will teach them even better.

Reasonable Expectations

Even when we are at our very best, all any child can learn is his one year's worth.

To say, "The kindergarten (or nursery school or day care or Head Start) teaches reading" must not mislead us into unreasonable expectations. Nor must we mislead the public. Under-six education must teach all the subject matters, but this cannot mean that the child learns them once and for all. No level of education — not education over-six or under-six — ever teaches all there is to know about anything. It simply teaches one year's worth.

A freshman in college takes a course in literature. If it has been a good course, he has learned a freshman year's worth. He has studied literature before. He studied it in nursery school and in kindergarten because these levels teach literature. He studied it in elementary and secondary school. And now in college he studies it again, and he will go on and on. There is American Literature and English Literature and World Literature. There is the literature of special periods: Writers of the Eighteenth Century, the Romantic Novels .... the literature of special styles of writing: prose, poetry, drama.... There are intensive courses in the writings of one author or another: Shakespeare, Emerson, Molière .... The freshman has only scratched the surface. He has learned this one year's worth. The study of literature enriched his living in that year. What more could one ask? Of a college year, a nursery school year, a kindergarten year?

Learning starts early and must go on and on. This need for continuity is increasingly being recognized in the teaching of reading. It is absurd to think of children as learning to read in first grade. A child learns a first grade's worth in first grade. Then he has to continue learning more in all the years to come: to read with greater speed; with greater ability to cope with new words; with better understanding and more critical comprehension; to read foreign languages, to read shorthand, to read technical literature. Reading specialists say: "We have to teach reading every year, on through high school and college, and teach it in every subject — history, science, mathematics...."

The continuity of learning stands out in some non-school fields. A mother carries her five-month-old in her arms as she stands in the waves at the seashore, the water up to her knees. This mother is teaching her child to swim. This is a very beginning lesson —

a lesson in enjoying the water, a lesson in not being afraid. Don't ever minimize the beginning lessons.

The same child, three years later, builds sand castles at the water's edge. Now the waves lap up and touch his knees. He is still learning to swim. Swimming instruction does not begin when a child first ducks his head or first practices his kick. These are simply stages in a continuous instructional process. Nor does learning to swim end when the child finally thrashes and splashes for twenty-five yards. This, too, is one stage. It was preceded by many lessons; many more are still to come.

In every field there are foundational learnings. There are the early beginner's learnings; there are the highly specific, advanced, more technical and detailed learnings of the "graduate" student — in swimming, and in the humanities and mathematics and the sciences and the social sciences.

Good instruction teaches as much as the student can master at the time. Good instruction uses methods that are right for the student at the time. The amount learned differs with age and with the child. But the instruction is all within the basic field. The five-month-old is studying swimming. Three-year-olds study reading. Three-, four-, five-year-olds study Anthropology, Arithmetic, Arts, Astronomy . . . right on down through the Z's. And they will learn as much as a three- or four- or five-year-old can in one year.

Parents can see the logic of this if we meet with them and if they have a full, open chance to talk out all their doubts and questions. This is especially true if they know all that is going on in a rich and stimulating classroom. But if we leave parents to flounder on their own, evaluation will continue to mean a reading readiness test, and reading readiness exercises will remain the core of the curriculum.

The Measurable and the Meaningful

Another reason for the inadequacy of evaluation in under-six education is the heavy reliance on objective evaluative instruments. Americans like to come out with a score, a grade, a number, a percentile. This seeming precision is one of the reasons why reading readiness tests sound better to many people than the "test" of a child's actual reading behavior, even though the artificial tests utterly fail to measure desire as a part of readiness. The love for the sound of precision is a reason why research evaluating the efficiency of Head Start or the impact of kindergartens turns to tests that measure vocabulary and IQ and items of factual knowledge, instead of in-depth studies of individuals and their families.

There is nothing wrong with objective tests *except* ... there are too few tests available and the ones available often measure the wrong things. Yet we stay wedded to objective instruments. The easy availability of the wrong tests gives us empty answers, but we persist in using them.

The tests we have and go on using tell us whether or not a child has learned to distinguish a triangle from a rectangle and whether or not he knows the right word for each figure. The tests are no help in telling us whether or not the youngster has been made more dependent in the process, whether he has been made more competitive, whether his hostility to adults has increased, whether he has been made more conforming or insincere, whether he sees himself more as stupid or brilliant or unimportant . . . . We know whether or not he can give the right answer, but we have no objective evaluative techniques for revealing whether or not the right answer has made him a better person, better able to live with himself and better for all the rest of us to live with. The devotion to objective evaluative techniques makes us confuse the measurable with the meaningful.

We are like the man, down on his hands and knees, searching under the street light for his lost wristwatch. A helpful policeman joins the search, but when they are unsuccessful the policeman finally asks: "Are you sure you lost it here?" "Oh, no," the man replies, "I lost it up the street but the light is better here."

Evaluation of early education has to center on the goals of under-six education. These are twofold. *For the individual,* as stated on page 3, early education aims "to help children learn, and to do it in such a way that the youngsters live their years of ages three and four and five in the richest, most satisfying, most constructive manner possible. The one big job (of nursery school, kindergarten, day care, Head Start), once a child is enrolled, is *to teach* so that each youngster is more glad he is alive during these early years." This ultimate concern is the quality of the child's living at the time, his sense of self-fulfillment.

For our society, early education aims to develop boys and girls with the qualities our country most needs. It seeks to produce people such as rugged individualists, free people, people who will use their heads and have a heart. The second ultimate concern is the development of human attributes, the qualities that make up the person.

A year's growth in any subject, the mastery of any skill, the addition of any knowledge are all important — but these are not the end goals. Subject matter is the means through which we work. The goals — evaluation has to center on them — are a very different thing. We must not let the availability of objective instruments in some few areas sidetrack us. We must not let their availability make us concentrate on measuring our means while we ignore the end results we really seek.

Subjectivity

The easy availability of objective tests and the lure of the shiny scores they yield need not force us into measuring the wrong outcomes. We can continue to use intelligence tests and vocabulary tests for the help they provide in understanding individuals — but at the same time we can use, much more fully than we ever have, subjective measures as our major evaluative tools.

Subjectivity has its pitfalls, as do the objective approaches. But subjective measures have one overriding virtue: They free us to evaluate what under-six education is all about. They free us to examine the quality of a child's living; they free us to look at his qualities as a human being. They do not force us into focusing on side issues or tangents.

We have been needlessly scornful of subjectivity and afraid of it. We have been halfhearted and hesitant about using it. We have underplayed the value of observation by humans and overprized the importance of a machine's score or number or grade. We need to appreciate more the value of concerned-parent and trained-teacher insight. We especially need to create better machinery so these insights can operate.

Teachers live with a child in school. Parents live with him at home. The shared observations of these two sets of people add up to a sensitive evaluative instrument for gauging a child's state of mind. Does he seem alive and alert? Does he seem vigorous? Does he seem enthusiastic and responsive? Is he eager to come to school? When he returns to his home is he fussy, fighty, tense? Does he act, school and home, as if he is operating on all of his cylinders, or does he seem to be dragging through his days: bored, untouched, apathetic? It is not difficult for people who live close to a child to assess how he is feeling about his life. There is no reason to downgrade this assessment — this is the important job to be done and parents and teachers can do it.

We do need better machinery through which to do it, however. We need major blocks of time for parent-teacher conferences, regularly throughout the year. We need the continuous flow of communication through brief, informal telephone and face-to-face conversations. Evaluation is not a job for June. If we wait until then, too often we will only be able to look back in anger and in dismay. Our communication system must be so open that parents and teachers can galvanize into thought and action the minute a signal comes, from home or school, that a youngster is not full of zest.

We also need a framework, a common focus as we observe children and as we talk together. Both parents and teachers must understand what matters most to children during these early years. There is an urgent job to be done here in the nursery-kindergarten-day care-Head Start room meetings. Building a deep awareness of the basic growth tasks young children face ought to have a top place on the agenda of these room meetings.

Sharing this top billing should be the discussions on the kind of human our society needs, presented in Chapter 3. These two items — the basic growth needs of children, the qualities our society prizes — give parents and teachers a solid framework for their evaluative conferences together.

Basic Growth Tasks

The basic growth tasks are the child's private learnings. They are the meaning he takes from all that happens to him. They are what he learns about people, about the world into which he has been born, about himself — over and beyond whatever else we teach him. These learnings are the ones most apt to be remembered. They are the learnings that will most affect how a child feels and what he does in every future situation.

In the under-six years all young children work to discover how much trust they can put in adults and, in turn, how much safety there is in their world. This search for a sense of trust is a basic growth task, one uppermost in the child's mind. It is the first meaning he takes from how he is handled and treated in every little event at home. As he moves on into a group this remains the lesson of prime importance: What are big people like? The poorest child searches for answers, the most privileged child searches. Without good adults the world looks mighty scary to the very young, to all of them. And it can stay a scary-looking place.

In the under-six years all young children work to discover ways of living with their own age-mates. The search is a complicated one that causes deep pain and hurt, just as it brings sweet rewards. It is a fumbling process of trial and error and experimentation. It is a slow process and a delicate one. The child must feel more fully himself as he builds his wider social bonds, not less true to himself because he is socialized. Young children are at the start of a lifelong process of finding out more about how to live with their own generation and with older and younger people. This is a matter of consuming importance, a growth task that they are aware of all of the time at home and at school.

In the under-six years all young children want to grow in their own powers, too. The child is born dependent, but no child wants to stay that way. He is curious about the world in which he finds himself. He wants to understand and increasingly to manage that world. He wants to build mastery over his own body, the very first house he lives in. He wants to develop skill in spoken language so that he can further control his environment. He faces the especially difficult task of developing emotionally. Without an expanding range of emotions the child's life stays thin, empty, meagre. Without expanding control over the expression of emotion the child's life is turbulent, troublesome to the rest of us and frightening to the child.

Young children need strong, helpful big people to care for them for many years. But during all these years they seek to feel strong and powerful so that they can care for themselves. The child seeks to discover that *he* is good. He can hold his head up. He *is* somebody. He can manage in this world.

The young child's search for trust in adults, his search for joy in his age-mates, his search for confidence in himself, is called the development of his self-concept. The child is "a nothing" at birth. He must move from that nothingness. The whole point of his living, its very significance, lies in his movement toward self-concept.

Healthy self-concept means dignity. It means the child becomes a person, alive with a full feeling of self-awareness, self-direction.

This is what children come to school to learn: *Selfhood.* Proud selfhood and the development of the special qualities our society needs are what evaluation has to focus on. Parents and teachers, pooling their thinking, must both come to see these as crucially important — not reading readiness, not getting ready for first grade, not countable, isolated language or intelligence test scores.

Anecdotal Records

Teachers, more than parents, can collect written evidence which bears on these central goals. Anecdotal records, brief descriptions of behavior, can provide specifics for discussion as parents and teachers confer. In the busyness of a day a teacher may need some prop to make herself keep records — the job can so easily be overlooked. One technique is to set a concrete goal of writing up every day a fixed number of behavioral incidents: two or three or four. The exact number makes no difference, but some set number can help to fix the pattern of writing down the specific happenings so that they are not forgotten. Another aid is to carry a pad and pencil tucked in one's pocket. Still another: Preserve some minutes for record time, immediately after the children leave, when the incidents are still fresh in your mind.

Such anecdotal records, incidentally, become an excellent means of spotting children who are being overlooked — at the end of a period you discover that you have no records on some of them at all! Anecdotal records are also a means of discovering whether or not some areas of development are being overlooked. You have records galore on social behavior but hardly any that reveal intellectual or physical or emotional response.

Anecdotal records can be supplemented by planned and scheduled observations of each child. There ought to be spot-checks from time to time, with a full recording of what a youngster does for fifteen or twenty minutes, as if a motion picture camera were making a documentary of how the child spends those minutes of his life. November's documentary compared with February's documentary can throw light on whether a child's behavior is expanding or whether he seems to be standing still.

Conferences, conversations, meetings, anecdotal records, planned observation — all mean added work for the teacher. There is no getting away from it. Much of this can only be done when there are two teachers to a group, a teacher and an aide. Much can only be done when class size is right for the age. But unless we actively and aggressively seek evidence on the measures that count, we will everlastingly be at the mercy of the easy evidence on the measures that count less.

5

The Tools and The Freedom to Teach

Many teachers know how to build a good program for children. They understand child development; they hold good democratic goals; they have a rich cultural background and they know good teaching methods *but*: Their hands are tied. They are blocked from using all they know. External pressures determine their curriculum, not good theory.

Teachers are frustrated by these external pressures. Too many good teachers leave the profession in despair. Too many of the teachers who stay are worn down by the circumstances under which they work.

To get a good program for young children the first step often is to tackle these external pressures. Until they are licked, theory never has a chance to operate. Overcoming them must have A-1 priority.

CLASS SIZE

The strongest of the malignant pressures is large class size. There is no more pernicious obstacle to a thoughtfully planned program.

Large class size is a roadblock to meeting individual differences.

Large class size is a roadblock to working with parents.

Large class size is a roadblock to an activity program of first-hand experiencing, of learning by doing. It limits the kinds of experiences that can be opened up. It rules out all those activities that make a muss, those that call for much teacher supervision, those that create any noise.

Large class size limits children's choices. It cuts down on their movement, their conversation, their social give-and-take.

Large class size makes teachers talk more *at* children. It forces teachers to give more commands. It leads to lining up, to waiting. It breeds more all-group activities; it cuts down on the number of small-group and individual experiences.

Large class size makes us pretend that young children are older than they are. It spawns teaching methods that are inappropriate and goals that are inappropriate.

Large class size spoils everything.

Until we lick the problem of large class size we will never have nursery schools or kindergartens or day care centers or Head Start programs of which we can be proud.

Standards for Class Size

Research cannot prove that any one class size is the optimum for all educational experiences. Class size is relative. It depends on the age of the children, the methods of teaching, the goals of the classroom. Graduate seminars often are limited to three or five students; college lectures commonly serve several hundred students.

There are, however, clear, almost unanimous guides to right class size that have accumulated over the years from the practical, personal experience of teachers of young children. The result of this experience has been written into law in those states that regulate private nursery schools and kindergartens. It has set the standard for the very best private schools, those which strive with high tuition and endowment to achieve high quality education.

Good class size — not small class size but *right* class size — for three-year-olds is about 12 children in a group with two teachers, a trained head teacher and a teacher's aide.

Good class size for four-year-olds is about 16 children in a group with two teachers, a trained teacher and a teacher's aide.

Good class size for five-year-olds is about 20 children in a group. Fives — so like fours and threes — also need two teachers, a trained head teacher and a teacher's aide. A paid aide in a public kindergarten of 20 children is a rarity. A volunteer aide should not be.

The Head Start standard — 15 children to a classroom with a trained teacher, a teacher's aide, and volunteers — seems right for disadvantaged five-year-olds. These children have intensified needs; Head Start is compensatory education. This standard is too high, however, when Head Start serves four-year-olds — the number of children to a classroom then should be about 12. When Head Start moves down the age scale, as it probably will, to serve three-year-olds, 10 should be the maximum number of children.

The class size for day care centers should be the same as in nursery schools and kindergartens, depending on the age of the children. The number of paid adults must be somewhat greater, however, because of the longer hours of operation of the day care center. Usually one trained head teacher, one full-time teacher's aide, one part-time teacher's aide, and volunteers can do the job well.

We are all so accustomed to mobs in the classroom that these standards are bound to seem idealistic. For instance the standard of 20 children in a kindergarten classroom inevitably seems starry-eyed. Our good private kindergartens have had to meet this standard, but we have let the public kindergarten standard slip very badly through the years. Teacher after teacher feels: "I'm lucky this year . . . . I only have 35." And she means 35 × 2 — morning and afternoon! The long history of slippage may make some compromise a necessary transitional step. Good education could compromise on 25 five-year-olds in a kindergarten — but there should be no compromise on staffing. Kindergartens need two adults; they need one paid professional teacher and one aide, paid or unpaid, parent or non-parent — especially if there are 25 youngsters.

These standards do not reflect the prevailing situation. But the standards are right — it is the situation that is wrong! *What is* distorts our efforts for children. We cannot go on forever accepting as right and necessary what we are now doing. Public education must not be equated with second-rate education. It must become good education — not luxurious, not frilly, but right for the age.

Solutions for Class Size

Sometimes the solution is right at hand, *if* the overcrowding results from a shortage of space and from our insistence on squeezing all of our children into the "official" school building. Sometimes we have the money for teachers and for equipment but we don't have the room. Fortunately, five-year-olds are seldom disadvantaged — and sometimes very advantaged — by being housed in a portable or a temporary building on the school grounds or in an off-campus location such as a rented home or store or other building which has been converted to kindergarten use. If lack of space within the school is the sole cause of overly large class size there should be no hesitancy about dividing groups into smaller sections and using such auxiliary facilities to achieve right class size.

See pages 148-149 for a discussion of the positive gains in housing a kindergarten in its own small, separate building. One word of caution, however: An aide is imperative, not a luxury in any sense, when a group is housed in a building by itself.

Unfortunately, too often the problem is lack of space *and* lack of teachers and equipment and money — a total shortage of general support. Teachers must be active citizens working and voting to bring about adequate federal and state and local support for under-six education. Only one area of general education has succeeded in persuading legislatures and the public of the necessity for right class size. Special Education — the education of the mentally retarded, the physically handicapped, the emotionally disturbed — seemingly has won the battle. Those of us in early education have to do more than we have done to help people see that the education of the child under six is also "special" education.

While we are working for adequate support there are also in-between steps we can take. These are not solutions — only more money can solve the basic problem. And these in-between steps are palliatives; they bring new problems of their own. But they can, however, help tide us over until there is good financial support. Teachers of young children would do well to persuade principals, superintendents, and members of Boards of Education to experiment with these ideas, when class size gets out of hand.

Drop-out Days

One technique for creating right class size is the device of Drop-out Days.

Customarily children come to school five days a week. Schools run from Monday through Friday. This arrangement is good *if* the enrollment is 12 in a three-year-old group, 16 in a four-year old group, 20 in a five-year-old group (or 25, if you are compromising.)

When enrollment is higher the Drop-out Day approach says: "We're sorry. We don't have room for everyone five days a week. We can provide a good kindergarten program only four days a week." Each day one-fifth of the children will not attend. The total enrollment in the kindergarten is 30, but each day one-fifth of the children will have Drop-out Day — the actual enrollment will be 24, within the range of compromise. Some children will come Monday, Tuesday, Wednesday, Thursday; they drop out Friday. Some come Tuesday, Wednesday, Thursday, Friday; they drop out Monday. And so it goes.

If the enrollment is 35 or 40, as it unfortunately frequently is, each child has two Drop-out Days. He comes to kindergarten only three days a week, but when he comes the class size is right.

The result is a clear definition: A kindergarten is a group for about 20 five-year-olds (or about 25, if the compromise is made). When the number exceeds that we have a mob scene — we no longer have a kindergarten.

Drop-out Days are not as revolutionary as they sound. It is true that public education has had a proud tradition. We don't turn children away—we have open doors. The youngsters usually come pouring in. This general policy of non-exclusion entitles us to a glorious A for Effort, but it often leads to a D in Achievement. Although the policy is well established, there have been exceptions when there are shortages of money or teachers or space. The two-session kindergarten is one such exception. Almost all five-year-olds now "drop out" half a day every day! The two-shift and three-shift elementary and secondary schools are exceptions; these mean shorter hours and less attendance than the "normal." The idea is not brand new.

Drop-out Days are not popular with teachers. The continuity of a program is stymied. One-fifth, sometimes two-fifths of the children miss the Tuesday trip to the turkey farm — Tuesday is not their day for school. This discomfort to teachers may not be all bad, however. We need the pinpricks of Drop-out Days to prod us to work more vigorously for adequate financial support. We have learned to put up with the discomforts of large class size. We have learned to close our eyes and our minds to what crowds make us do to children. Drop-out Days cause some distortion of their own, but at least they remind us of the basic problem. That problem is the overly large class size that makes the Drop-out Day necessary.

Drop-out Days also shock parents. Initially parents often have a blind, angry response, hitting out at school people: "My child is school age — you must take him!" But parents can understand, if we help them through meetings and conferences, that school personnel do not set the tax rate. Schools are the people's schools. The people determine how good those schools will be, how extensive their offerings will be, how high a quality they will have. The school in effect is simply saying: "We are sorry. You have only given us enough tax money to have a three-day or a four-day kindergarten." It is raising the question: "Is this what you really want?"

We are shielding parents today. We keep them from knowing what actually goes on within our classrooms. Parents send their children in all good faith. The children come to school, the parents stay home, and parents never know that their tax money is insufficient. They never know that they are buying a kindergarten in name only. The anger and upset of a community is distressing and difficult to live with. But without the deep concern of parents, schools never become truly great.

Drop-out Months

Varying the number of months in the school year is another, probably better, expedient for achieving right class size. Usually children come to school Monday through Friday, September through June. When class size is not right we can say: "We are able to take your child from September to January. Those four months will have to be his 'kindergarten year'." Or the period might be September through February or whatever adjustment is needed so that at any one time there are only about 20 to 25 five-year-olds enrolled.

These are not Drop-out Days but *Drop-out Months*. A child attends continuously, Monday through Friday. The program has continuity during that time. But each child has a shorter school year so that he can go to a real kindergarten during that shorter year.

Drop-out Months also are not new. Our school year varies now in different parts of the country. In the near future those communities most committed to good education may lengthen their school year to eleven or twelve months. The school year is not a God-given arrangement — it is purely man-made. At the kindergarten level, in particular, the shorter school year is unfortunately very common. Many school systems which have no regular public kindergarten program do have summer groups. They cannot or will not provide ten months of kindergarten education — they provide two months.

Summer Head Start is the most obvious example of Drop-out Months. Its children come only eight weeks. They "drop out" all the rest of the time. No one thinks that eight weeks is long enough. It is sheer compromise. Children with disadvantaged backgrounds ought to have twelve-month schooling, and not simply for the year before their entrance into "regular" school. But Summer Head Start turned to the in-between, temporary answer, to the palliative. Eight weeks of something good seemed better than ten months of overcrowded education, and better than none at all.

There is always the danger that people will forget that short programs — Drop-out Days or Drop-out Months — are only expedient strategy. It would be easy for our country to assume that Head Start was meant to be and always must be primarily a summer program. It has been easy for many communities to live

with their abbreviated summer kindergartens. There is the additional danger that summer programs, in particular, will strain to
compress into their brief span all that regular-length programs
can do. Their summer placement accentuates the idea that kindergarten "gets children ready for first grade." It hides the fact that
kindergarten is primarily to make the fifth year of life more worth
living.

There are no perfect solutions, short of solving the basic
problem. We cannot simultaneously have inadequacies in support
and fully adequate programs. Some price must be paid by somebody, somewhere, somehow. The highest price tag comes with
overly large class size — we have to remember that. Any difficulties
that flow in the wake of expedients to meet this threat are less
serious than the difficulties that come from the main threat itself.

Teacher Aides

There should be an aide in every classroom for young children,
even when class size is right. Sound standards say: 12 three-year-
olds to *two* adults; 16 four-year-olds to *two* adults; 20 (or if need
be, 25) five-year-olds to *two* adults. But aides are seldom found
in public kindergartens except when class size mounts catastroph-
ically. This is a shame.

Some school people mistakenly think they have established good
working conditions when they provide two adults for 40 five-year-
olds. They are blind to how grievously they have compromised
the standards for right class size. The best that can be said is
that they have taken a slight step in the right direction — 40
children with two adults is better than the same number with
only one. But we have to learn not to wait until class size gets
completely out of hand before turning to this expedient. The
teacher with 20 five-year-olds should have an aide. But when the
number soars to 21 — it should not have to zoom to 40! — we
should not hesitate a second to find a paid or unpaid helper.

We have been discouragingly slow in bringing aides into the
public school kindergarten. The idea is old hat in the nursery
school, the day care center and now in Head Start (although
always in these instances with right class size). The cooperative
nursery school, in particular, has shown how well parents can

serve as aides. Co-ops for years have used parents as their assistant teachers and as assistants in every aspect of the program: shopping for supplies, office work, nursing services, repairs and maintenance. In a cooperative nursery school parents pay tuition but they also pay through their services. Each day the trained teacher, tuition-supported, is in charge; one assistant teacher — a parent, whose services are contributed — is her aide.

The origin of the cooperative idea stemmed from the same old irritant that confronts all under-six education: the ever-present lack of money. Parents wanted nursery education for their children but they could not afford to buy what a good classroom must have. They were short on cash, but not short on time and talent and concern. Many side-benefits have kept the idea strong and flourishing. Parent-participants understand their children better; they understand the processes of education better; they find personal growth and challenge through the fuller use of their abilities.

It is sheer waste if we continue to limit the idea of unpaid parent participants as teacher aides to cooperative nursery schools. The idea is fully applicable to public school kindergartens.

Head Start has opened up still more possibilities. It, too, uses parents as teacher aides, and also other residents of the poverty area being served. For reasons inherent in the war on poverty the aide in a Head Start classroom is paid. Head Start has gone beyond one aide, however. It has tapped many additional volunteers and has shown how non-parent volunteers can help in a program. Preadolescent boys and girls have worked effectively, giving their services to the program. So too have non-parents from the immediate neighborhood and from the whole community. The young, the older, the aging have all pitched in.

Head Start and co-ops have capitalized on a significant truth: There is talent in our population. We have a vast reservoir, especially of able women who are not using all they have to give at home or in business. Public education has created this wealth. Public education ought to take advantage of its own creation.

The experience of both programs shows another thing: People want to help. The mechanization and impersonalization of our society pushes too many of us to the sidelines. Humans have a hunger to be needed, a hunger to contribute to a worthwhile cause. It may come as a surprise that people do not resent being asked to help. The fact is: They are grateful for the opportunity.

Aides in the classroom create problems, of course. Aides — paid or unpaid — must be oriented to the jobs they are to do and oriented to the children. Conferences must be scheduled after a day's work or a week's work, looking back at what has happened and planning ahead. Differences of opinion are bound to arise. Lines of authority must continually be clarified. Personality differences crop up. On occasion individual volunteers or parent participators or paid aides do not work out; someone must handle the always difficult job of discharging a helper. Volunteers must be "disciplined." They need to understand that they cannot be casual or late or absent simply because they are not being paid. They must understand that they have volunteered for a real job. The teacher must discipline herself, too. It is easy to palm off all the dirty jobs on aides, easy to neglect to help them see the significance of their contribution, easy to give them the empty feeling of simply being used.

To avoid the inevitable human problems, clearly the only way is to "go it alone" and have only yourself to think of — allow no other adult in the classroom who has to be taken into account. A more constructive approach is to recognize the very pleasant side of working with an aide. It is like family life, and family living is usually the most rewarding kind. You have to talk things over. You have to take the teammate's point of view into account. You give a little but you gain a lot.

We must end the foolish notion that one teacher can teach a classroom of young children, even a class of right size. A program becomes outstandingly better whenever there is more than one head, more than one set of eyes and ears, more than one pair of hands and feet. The best advice one can give a teacher of young children who has the right class size but who works alone is: Get yourself a helper! Get a paid aide if you can, or an unpaid volunteer. Get parents. Get other adults. Get older children and adolescents. Get one helper. Get two if you can. No one teacher alone can do everything that a sensitive and stimulating program calls for.

This good advice to the teacher with right class size becomes almost an imperative when class size is overly large and cannot be reduced.

Three Less Wise Approaches

Waiting lists are another way of achieving decent class size. The obvious difficulty is that of determining who shall be admitted and who shall have to wait. "First come, first served" up to the limit of 12 or 16 or 20-25 can lead to unseemly competition among parents. It is also a dangerous approach if it means that the already privileged children of the most conscientious parents always come in first.

In a sense Head Start operates on a waiting-list basis, but one with a reverse twist. Its economic criterion for admission means that Head Start serves first those who need the experience most. Communities could, with justice, follow this reverse twist; they could use economic level or psychological or developmental status or any other criterion of need they wanted to establish. Most such standards, however, would require expensive, skilled, individual testing and would probably yield results difficult for a community to understand and accept.

Increasing the space to fit the overly large class size is another common but inadequate solution. Overflowing kindergartens are moved to the gymnasium, to the stage of the auditorium, to a ballroom — but the increased space seldom hits at the heart of the problem. The basic question is: How many other humans can the young child tolerate? With large class size, no matter how large the room, over-stimulation and over-excitement and distraction mount. No matter how large the room, the young child needs the personalization that can come only with right class size. The space standard — preferably 45-50 square feet per child — can mean lowering the size of the group if space is lacking, but if you had all the space in the world it should not mean increasing the size of the group to fit the space.

The third, least sensible approach of all is to *raise the school entrance age*. A school can reduce its eligible kindergarten population for one year by changing the entrance age from 4.9 to 5. The improvement in class size is obviously very temporary. The solution, however, seems so simple that school after school hopefully asks: "What is the right school entrance age?" The answer by this time ought to be clear: "Most children are ready for school by about the age of three, if the school is ready for them." This answer seldom comforts those who want to raise the school entrance age.

FIRST GRADE READING

Almost on a par with overly large class size as a skewing force on under-six education is the heavy-handed way in which reading is taught in first grade.

There are as many methods of teaching reading as there are school-book publishers. Unfortunately almost all of these methods have the same characteristics: They ignore individual differences, and they make children give up a part of being age six. The children must be quiet. They must sit to learn. First grade becomes a deadly serious book-centered study hall. Reading is a separate, isolated subject matter which has nothing to do with the activities of the children. A child learns to read from a commercially produced book, used nationwide. He learns the approved words or sounds or letters in a step-by-step progression.

The methods all pay lip service to individual differences. Everyone claims to recognize that children will be ready for intensive help in reading at different times. But in common practice the real message is clear: Tough luck if you happen to be a late starter or a slow grower... We understand but you fail! First grades tend to have a fixed grade standard. A child either comes up to snuff or the roof falls in.

Obviously it is difficult for teachers of children under six to influence what is done at the over-six ages. But until changes are made in the teaching of first grade reading under-six education faces two sorry alternatives: 1) We can fail children in kindergarten to save their failing in first grade; 2) We can make the same error first grades make — we can ignore individual differences and exert pressure to get each and every child ready for intensive reading instruction.

Difficult as the job is, realism says: If you want to improve programs in nursery school or kindergarten or day care or Head Start, you have to think about first grade. To protect our own programs, under-six teachers need to know the promising practices in the education that lies immediately ahead and give these whatever support is possible in whatever ways are open to us.

Individualized Reading

Any method of teaching reading in first grade that honestly takes individual differences into account will lift some of the weight off under-six education. Individualized Reading is one such promising practice.

In Individualized Reading each child chooses his own reading books in terms of his interests and his assessment of his own reading ability. A classroom offers the widest possible choice ranking from pre-primers and primers to teacher-made books to trade books. There is a reading time each day but the children seldom come together in groups. Each child chooses what to read and reads by himself. The teacher works with youngsters individually, although not with each child every day. She notes a child's weaknesses and his problems and makes suggestions that are a prescription for him alone. She notes his interests and opens up possibilities of new books that are especially right for him alone.

One good book describing Individualized Reading in more detail is Principles and Practices of Teaching Reading, 2nd Edition *by Arthur W. Heilman (Columbus, Ohio: Charles E. Merrill Publishing Company, 1967), pp. 341-371.*

Individualized Reading is the logical extension of the most prevalent present effort in first grades to take individual differences into account. Once first graders all read from the same page of the same book; the whole class was on the same word and the same line. The breakaway from this mass approach came when we divided children into at least three reading groups. Three groups are better than one. Twenty "groups" — each child reading on his own — is a still more sensitive step ahead. One child's reading level may be simply that of looking at the pictures in books; but he "reads" at his speed at his own desk, unembarrassed, unpressured, unashamed. Another youngster in the same first grade reads quickly and with understanding a book customarily read by third graders. He too is at his own desk, not held back, unhindered, going at his own speed and in the area of his interests.

Individualized Reading is so logical a "next step," so sensibly rooted in everyone's awareness of how different children are, that it is catching on. Individualized Reading marries some specific teaching methods more easily than others, but it is compatible with a wide range of approaches: with phonics, the Initial Teaching Alphabet, with linguistic approaches, with learning whole words. It is essentially a form of class organization rather than one particular teaching method.

There are some problems. Teachers and parents feel jittery because the teacher cannot hear every child read every day. The child reads but the teacher does not hear him. Some teachers feel more important when they have a reading group. They have more management to do; there is more limelight for the teacher. Individualized Reading requires skilled teachers with a keen ear for a child's problem, with a keen knowledge of materials that will lead him on. Ordinarily the publisher does much of this hard work for teachers through the teacher's manuals and the graded difficulty of the basic readers. An economic factor that militates against Individualized Reading is the need for a huge collection of varied materials. Publishers make less money and book salesmen must work harder on individual sales of individual books than they do with mass adoptions and bulk orders. Individualized Reading is catching on but it has not swept the country.

We shall all benefit as Individualized Reading grows in popularity. A child headed for such a program does not need to be "readied." His first grade teacher takes him as she finds him and helps him move on from there. No one has to jump through hoops to prepare him. Individualized Reading frees the nursery school and kindergarten and day care center and Head Start teacher to do what the first grade teacher does: To take their children as they find them and help them move on from there. This is not pressure, this is challenge. This is not distortion, this is teaching.

Language-Experience Approach

Any approach to functional reading in first grade — any method that does not demand that children give up their essential nature in order to learn — will take some of the heat off under-six education. The method of teaching reading that is most in line with this goal is usually called the Language-Experience Approach.

The Language-Experience Approach is an activity-centered way of teaching. The children must first be involved in significant experiences in the sciences, in the social sciences, in the arts or humanities. Then their reading grows out of the things they do. Reading is not isolated. It is not set apart, off in the blue. Reading is the inherent, symbolic aspect of real-life activities. The charts, the letters, the stories, the reports growing out of the activities become the child's primers.

The Language-Experience Approach allows youngsters to be active, busy, social, independent humans. It allows them to be the distinct individuals they are. Each child does as much reading and at whatever level his development makes right for him. The crux is the activity, not some preconceived, mass-packaged kind of reading. A group of six-year-olds will visit a newspaper office. On their return some will read the exciting fiction and non-fiction that centers around newspaper work. Others will dictate their own stories. The children all read at their developmental level but for all of them — as for three- and four- and five-year-olds — the experience is central.

> *One book describing this approach to the teaching of reading is* Learning to Read Through Experiences *by Doris Lee and R. V. Allen (New York: Appleton-Century-Crofts, 1963).*

The Language-Experience Approach to the teaching of reading is not new. It is as old as the activity school, at least as old as the 1920's. One cannot say, as one can about Individualized Reading: The idea is catching on. But the idea does not die. The teaching of reading is so emotionally charged — and such great financial stakes are involved — that school systems go backwards and forwards, making little gains, suffering little losses.

One thing is clear, however: Under-six education will be more free to do its job whenever any steps are taken in the direction of letting six-year-olds be active children, involved in projects, free to talk and move about, free to use their hands and bodies, free to respond to the stimulus of real-life situations rather than simply to the printed symbols on a page.

The Ungraded Primary

One organizational change affecting reading is making headway and can help nursery schools, kindergartens, day care centers, and Head Start. This is the ungraded primary.

The heart of the ungraded primary is the abolition of fixed grade standards until the end of third grade. All children are not expected to reach a definite reading level at the end of first grade as a precondition for their promotion into second grade. There is, therefore, no equivalent expectation that all children will reach a definite level of reading ability at the end of kindergarten as a precondition for their promotion into first grade. No teacher — except the last — has to turn over a "finished product" to the next teacher. Children with differing developmental rates or with special problems have four years to reach the standard set for "promotion."

This search for larger blocks of time is the logical extension of a development which began many years ago. Grades became year-long units rather than divided into two: 1A with promotion and retention; 1B with promotion and retention; 2A, 2B and so forth. The gift of time is a tremendous aid in lifting off the classroom teacher's shoulders the load of tomorrow's expectations.

This gift of time is most fully experienced when the same teacher stays with her group for more than one year. The teacher has no reason to worry about next year's teacher — she herself is that teacher. In some ungraded primary programs the same teacher stays with the children two or three years, not unlike the old "little red school house" where the children had the same teacher for eight years.

Many fringe benefits flow from this continuity. The opportunity to build a continuing relationship with one teacher is very significant for younger children. Parent-teacher relationships are also usually improved when adults have a longer span in which to come to know each other. Continuity gives teachers a better chance to understand each child and to find the approaches to teaching that will be most effective with him.

Summer Head Start has brought some of this continuity to education. First grade teachers often are Head Start teachers during the summer months. Not all are gentled by the experience. Some carry with them down into Head Start all of their first grade expectations plus a frenzied determination to whip the children into shape before "regular school" begins. Many other first grade teachers, however, build a new sympathy for children as children. They develop a fresh awareness of the interrelationships between physical health and intellectual learning, between social and emotional health and learning. They appreciate the strengths

Head Start children have, and the lacks that the long years of poverty living have built into them. They learn to respect the efforts and strengths of parents who raise their children in poverty's grip. Their awareness of individual differences is deepened. These teachers carry up to their September first grades a fresh determination to make that grade child centered, right for all the children who come no matter what the children are like when the term begins.

It would be a real step ahead if full-day kindergarten teachers could remain with their youngsters through first grade. Nursery and kindergarten teachers in private schools would do well to explore the possibility of their staying with the same children over a two- or three-year span.

The carry-over of teachers, a wonderful fringe benefit, is not essential to the success of the ungraded primary, however. A change in attitude and expectation is. Success in reading — as an isolated subject matter which is not related to the children's activities — cannot remain the single goal of first grade. Unfortunately in some schools the name is changed but the goal stays the same. The beginning years of school are upgraded but they retain all the old pressures for reading. The new ungraded primary uses new groupings, it speaks of "ladders" for reading, but reading as a separate subject remains the one central core of the curriculum. When this happens, even under the new name the kindergarten teacher and the nursery school teacher face the same old charge "to get children ready."

Transition Groups

Not as promising as ungraded primaries for lifting pressure is the idea of transition groups. Children who have had a year of kindergarten but who are "not ready for first grade" — i.e. the first grade is not ready for them — are "promoted" to a transition group. Such groups come with many names. They all stand for a state of limbo. The child hasn't failed kindergarten; he hasn't been promoted to first grade. He is in . . . transition.

Transition groups could contribute a little to pressure-reduction if they were a temporary placement. Promotion to a transition group ought not necessarily mean that a child has lost a year of his life. If a youngster gains in his ability to meet "grade standards," whether through maturation or through special help, he should be able easily to leave his transition track and return to his original age-mates.

The more transition groups are an inflexible placement, the more they stand for failure in everyone's mind: the child, the parent, the kindergarten teacher. The old goal has to remain: Work to get the child up to first grade standard. The result is that kindergarten becomes a diluted first grade.

Pressure would also lift a little if the transition group were seen as a helping way station rather than a dumping ground. Whenever a child is not ready for first grade, no matter how unreasonable the standards of that grade may be, the child is different. His difference may be a perfectly normal, healthy kind of difference: slower maturation or strong, competing, constructive interests. The difference may stem from some troublesome source: a physical defect in hearing or vision, some emotional upset or social inadequacy. The difference may be one no one should tamper with; it may be something remediable; it may be a difference that cannot be corrected — one to which child and parents and school will have to make a permanent accommodation. A transition group at its best is a place for finding out. Fifteen children looked as if they could take the first grade that lies ahead; five seemingly could not. Why? Someone ought to know the answers and then do whatever is called for.

If transition groups are to serve this diagnostic-therapeutic "special study" purpose, their size must be quite small. Fifteen children would be a full class. Transition teachers must have easy access to supportive psychological, medical, and social welfare services. Given this study approach, the right class size, the needed back-up resources, a transition group would not be a failure-station. The existence of such a group could lessen the pressure on under-six education.

Unfortunately, these two standards — temporary placement, a diagnostic-therapeutic approach — are seldom met. The usual transition group simply staves off the failure that would come in regular first grade. This is settling for very little. Children fail, but not quite as obviously as they otherwise would; kindergartens still have to push for first grade standards, but not quite as doggedly as they would if no buffer state existed.

The Need for Dialogues

Whether or not there are helpful organizational arrangements, kindergarten and first grade teachers must talk together. A level of trust has to come into being which does not exist at the present time.

Kindergarten and first grade teachers ought to eat lunch together, where schedules make this possible. They ought to meet after school hours. They ought to ask for time in faculty meetings for joint planning. Somehow, on school time or on their own if need be, kindergarten and first grade teachers need to build a regional pact, an "early education common market" of ideas.

This community of interest must develop if under-six education is to serve as the school's DEW Line. But there is an additional need — one of common defense. Both levels of education experience severe pressure to concentrate on reading. Both add to these pressures through their own imagination. There is no conclusive evidence that direct drill on reading readiness in kindergarten makes any difference at all in later reading achievement. About 40% of America's five-year-olds do not go to kindergarten; their fifth year of life is bleaker for this but their later reading does not suffer. There is no conclusive evidence that direct drill on reading readiness in kindergarten makes any great difference even with disadvantaged children. What these youngsters need — what all children need — is a teacher who will look on them as total people, not simply as pre-reading creatures. There is a lot of reason to believe that even first grades need not center on reading in the way that they do in order to produce children who will be able to read and who will love to read.

No sharp developmental differences make the six-year-old a fundamentally changed child from the five-year-old. Nothing ought to be taken out of a well-equipped kindergarten room to turn it into a good first grade. New materials have to be added, materials have to be more complex, but you add on — you don't take away. First grades need blocks as much as kindergartens do, only more of them. First grades need dramatic play corners as much as kindergartens do. First grades need easels and workbenches and sand and clay, as much as kindergartens do. First grades need their own private outdoor play areas as much as kindergartens do. Given a chance many first grade teachers will say to their kindergarten friends: "You have exactly what I need: puzzles, toys, boards and boxes, dolls, a workbench, wheel toys . . . ." Kindergarten teachers will chime in: "And we need more of them!" Allied, working as a team, kindergarten and first grade teachers can have greater muscle in getting what both must have.

SCHOOL ADMINISTRATION

A third disruptive force hurting programs for young children is the widespread ignorance about early education among school administrators. This is *not* to say that administrators are stupid. They simply do not know. They obviously have shown wisdom and ability in other school jobs, but these almost always have related to older children. Very few principals have taught children under six. Very few have ever taken courses on the education of children under six. Principals have good heads on their shoulders and their hearts are in the right place. But nothing in their past prepares them for knowing the special needs of the very young.

Uninformed, it is easy for the administration to throw young children in with the mass. The children are school children now — they are old enough to be treated like all the rest. They have to walk quietly in the halls; this is what school children do. The kindergarten children have to come to school assemblies and wiggle through speakers, films, programs that are geared to fourth grade. Worse: The kindergarten class has to take its turn in putting on a performance for the PTA. The gross insensitivities are rationalized: "It makes them feel a part of the school" . . . "It helps them to feel big." The actual impact is to herd young children, to manipulate them. Youngsters learn their own smallness and impotence.

There are errors of omission. Kindergartens cannot get sand — no other group needs it, why should the five-year-olds? Kindergartens have no outdoor equipment — other groups use the bare playground, why should kindergarten be special? There are no workbenches. You can't cook in the classroom. Water play is too messy. Trips can be arranged only if the kindergarten has a lawyer to present its case and an expeditor to see the forms through bureaucratic channels.

There are errors of commission. Team teaching, which may have virtues for older age groups, is imposed on the kindergarten. The main result with five-year-olds is to bring too many young children together at once, and to segment the program into artificial subject-matter areas. Special teachers in art, music, physical education—valuable resources when working directly with older children — are imposed on the kindergarten. The result is that the day is splintered, and the specialists seldom know five-year-olds as well as the regular classroom teacher.

Sometimes administrative decisions are issued because there is a vacuum. No one objects. Teachers without guts do not question why or offer better alternatives. They do not even chafe under restrictive regulations. They may feel safer because of them, but their children chafe. Other teachers run scared. They translate "suggestion" into "requirement," "recommendation" into "regulation," "possibility" into "policy." They are unwilling to use the latitude that exists. They themselves narrow their own freedom.

Most teachers of young children are gentle souls. We are quiet. We are self-effacing. But if we stay too quiet the pressures pile up. A good teacher has to stand up and speak out for young children's needs. Without a spokesman for young children, school is school is school — but seldom a good school for five-year-olds.

Lobbying for Young Children

Many a teacher has found her own way of standing up for children. Her principal is persuaded that he has the best kindergarten teacher in the world. He wouldn't dream of making her do something that she didn't think was right. She is his expert on young children.

The key is the teacher's attitude. A good teacher respects the principal's position. He is "the boss." He is responsible for the school as a whole — responsible to the superintendent, through him to the Board of Education and to the public. The principal has the perspective that goes with this broader responsibility. But a good teacher also respects herself.

The principal is "the boss," but the teacher is the professional in her field. She is trained. She is a specialist. She has expertise. Most important today: She is rare. Good teachers of any age level who know their business are hard to find — good teachers of young children are especially precious. The teacher has every right to hold her head high, to feel a sense of dignity in the work she is doing. She has the right to assume — without the slightest doubt, unquestioningly — that her point of view and her ideas and her knowledge will, of course, be taken into account.

This does not mean that the teacher always wins the argument . . . at least, not the first time. But it does mean that the teacher has the fullest right to be heard. And the greatest obligation to speak up. It means that no one, arbitrarily or in an authoritarian way, has the right simply to tell the teacher what to do. A professional cannot be pushed around.

Those who have the courage to stand up for what is right for children combine charm with their courage. Making a case for young children's needs does not have to be a nasty business. The first step is to build friendly relationships with the school principal. The teacher's job is to woo him . . . professionally. No one can spell out all the ways of doing this. We each do it in our own way. But the important point is: Do it! It is easy to become so immersed in our work with children that we forget that the success of that work often depends on the goodwill of others.

Clever teachers of young children do not let the principal sit in his office holding his head because little children make so much noise. They don't wait until the administrator stalks into their classroom for a state visit. They think up every excuse to have "the boss" come to their room as often as possible: to say "Hello" to the children, to admire some block building, to share mid-morning juice. They want him to get used to the noise and the movement and the activity and the color and sound and smell of a kindergarten. Once the principal ventures in, the children become excellent ambassadors of goodwill. Especially if "the boss" is a man, he can be sure of a royal welcome.

Teachers think of myriad ways of making the program for young children reach out from their room into the principal's office. When the children bake cookies a plateful always goes to the principal, the gift borne by proud children who are very easy to like. Children dictate stories for the principal. Some of their prize pictures are mounted for his office. A lovely clay masterpiece is a gift for his desk. Like a Washington lobbyist, the teacher is not above "buying" a little friendship in high places.

Friends in Seats of Power

Public school principals, incidentally, are not the only ones who must become the targets of a "charm campaign." Ministers of churches which have weekday nursery schools sometimes are less than delighted with the mess and activity and noise of the group. Little in their theological study centered around the developmental needs and characteristics of children under six. There is no reason why they should know what young children are like . . . initially. But they can be helped to learn.

Bus drivers — the driver of the private nursery school or day care center pickup or the driver of the public school bus — are important targets. If the teacher does not help them to understand, they can do bad things when the children are in their care: yell at them, scare them, be gruff. And they can do bad things to the children when the youngsters are with you. Not understanding, drivers can so easily become rumormongers who whip up the pressures that swirl around your program: "The children are wild" . . . "There is no discipline" . . . "They don't learn a thing."

Custodians can make or break a program for young children. They can fuss endlessly over spills on the floor. They can seem to hide when heavy equipment has to be moved. They can turn sour and spread tales when equipment is broken. The same people, charmed, can so easily become scouts who spot cartons and boxes young children can use, and wheels and cans and wood that would otherwise be thrown away. They can so easily become heroes who delight in making minor repairs and who feel proud because they have helped a program move along. They can become strong advocates of activity because "they know" little children need to work and be busy. They know, because someone helped them to know.

The school secretary can speed newsletters to parents and other materials along the way . . . or block them forever. Whoever does the purchasing can make supplies and materials flow or get lost in the bureaucratic jungle. Especially in the day care center, all the food service people are important. Kitchen workers can welcome young children into their domain or they can be like their refrigerators — cold and icy.

Everyone tends to like little children. We have a lot going for us that can win support and interest and backing and enthusiasm. The battle is half won before we even begin — but winning the second half, going all the way, depends on our lobbying.

Sounder Educational "Campaigns"

Once in the good graces of their principal, many teachers set out to educate him. They are not even very subtle about it. They bring him a book or pamphlet on early childhood education. They give him marked copies of the professional journals in their field. Any number of teachers invite their principal to come along to a local or state or national meeting of the Association for Childhood Education International or the National Association for the Education of Young Children. At both associations' conferences it is not the least bit unusual to hear a principal say: "My teacher made me come." But it is very apparent that the principal is not the least bit sorry. Some smart teacher has helped the administrator feel that early education is his field, too.

Full understanding, of course, comes only through talks and discussions, face to face, with time to state positions and the reasons why. The teacher of young children must have as one of her theme songs: "I'm just a girl who *can* say 'No'." Or better still: "No, thank you." How about workbooks in the kindergarten? "No, thank you." Could the children put on a little show for the parents? "No, thank you." And "No, thank you" to films and assemblies in the auditorium and to a host of other bright ideas that are fine for older children.

"No, thank you . . . and I'll tell you why." Because the "No" cannot stem from isolation or sheer resistance or negativism or whim. The "No" has to be the occasion to make more clear what

young children are like; what will benefit them because they are the way they are; what will do them little good or even some harm because of their stage of development.

The response isn't always "No," of course. If something has to be done, it has to be done. But ways can usually be found of doing it so that young children benefit, instead of being hurt. The teacher of young children, the good shepherd of her flock, is imaginative in suggesting ways to adjust mass rules and regulations and school-wide procedures to fit the young. How can the entrance to school be handled so that it isn't a frightening or lonely time for little children? How can hearing tests and medical exams be done in the most personalized, least traumatic way? How can fire drills be managed so that young children are not terrified? How can young children get the benefit of special teachers without allowing these resources to become an intrusion on a program and a cause of undesirable rigidity?

In these dialogues the teacher is also the salesman, plugging away for new services and provisions that will especially benefit young children. These boys and girls need an outdoor play yard of their own, with their own special equipment. They need much greater freedom than other groups to take field trips. They must have a staggered start to school in September. Report cards that may be right for the upper grades can be very wrong for young children; their teacher must have ample time for conferences with parents. Young children need more than one teacher in their classroom — there has to be one aide at least, either paid or a volunteer. Young children should eat lunch in their classrooms, not in a crowded, noisy cafeteria. They need first claim on whatever psychological services exist so that problems can be nipped in the bud. They need bussing arrangements that are not fatiguing or frightening. Young children need toilet facilities that are homelike rather than institutional. They need rooms that are acoustically treated. They need arrangements for dressing and undressing and for hanging up their clothing that will foster their independence — crowded and pinched, high hallway lockers fit the older ages but not these children.

The needed equipment or supplies or space or arrangements will never come if the initiative rests with others. Not that others do not care — they often simply do not know. The teacher has to be the idea person, taking the lead in making a large public school right for its very smallest, youngest citizens.

Small, Separate Buildings

One administrative arrangement—the primary school—is slowly taking hold, making some of this lobbying and intensive "educating" of adults unnecessary. The primary school is an elementary school set apart, established specifically for the youngest children. Today's primary schools usually serve kindergarten children through second or third grade, and they sometimes include a Head Start group. The day may come when primary schools will extend down to nursery school and certainly include a day care center.

Primary schools frequently are ungraded. They frequently have their teachers stay with groups for more than one year. But their essence is: They are schools set apart. They are schools specifically for the youngest, whether "youngest" ends at grade 2 or grade 3.

Children gain directly by being in a small, separate building. There is less crowding, less herding, less confusion. The little school can be more tolerant of the noise young children make: the noise of their play, their conversation, their music, their carpentry. A separate building is more likely to have the outdoor space and equipment young children need, not the ball fields and courts and wide-open empty game spaces that are typical of total elementary schools. The errors of omission and of commission that occur when classes for younger children are added on below a regular elementary school are less likely to occur in the primary school. The younger children are *primary*, not afterthoughts.

The indirect advantages are equally important, however. The faculty is homogeneous — everyone who teaches in the school is an early childhood specialist. Everyone thinks and plans for young children. Of course, no law guarantees that the principal will be an early childhood specialist — some ex-high school football coaches become principals. But in a primary school the principal is more apt to be a former kindergarten or primary teacher and to have taken course work in early childhood education. Such a background does not automatically solve every problem or insure continuous smooth sailing. It does provide an excellent base for discussion and makes a sympathetic ear more likely to be present.

The growing interest in year-round Head Start and other compensatory programs for young children may lead to more primary schools. Many of these new programs, of necessity, are housed in temporary quarters — the existing public school does not have the room to take them under its wing. The new programs are found in portable and temporary facilities on a school playground. They are found in rented space in stores and converted residences. Some are in public non-school buildings: in libraries, recreation buildings, public housing. Some are in churches. These new "isolated" programs may be lucky, not disadvantaged, because of their separateness. The building they are in is expressly for the children who use it. The program does not have to be toned down or modified to meet the varying needs of many ages.

We do well to remember: Such separateness was one of the reasons for having nursery-kindergarten groups in the first place. The needs of young children conflicted with the needs of the older members who make up a home: older brothers and sisters, mothers and fathers, grandparents and visitors and guests. Sensitive parents sought a place young children could have as their own, a place where they could be themselves. This gain is threatened when programs for young children are housed in a multi-age elementary school, just as it was lost when young children spent all their time in a multi-age home.

Centralization

An opposite trend toward centralization also has momentum at the present time. The roots of this trend go back to the effort to do away with the one-room school house so that rural boys and girls could have the advantages of centralized services and wider social stimulation. Today's interest in centralization, however, is in our cities. There is talk of "educational parks" — large school centers of the highest quality, not located in neighborhoods but at central points throughout a city. Educational parks are seen as a possible means of ending low-quality ghetto schools, of ending the confining homogeneity when all children come from the same poverty area, and as a means of achieving constructive integration of racial and economic groups.

The need for improving the segregated inner city school is pressing. Unfortunately, the right solution is hard to find. If the case for educational parks rested solely on the benefits that come through centralized facilities, one could clearly say for young children: "No, thank you." The youngest do not need the facilities that come with bigness. The services of the central school — the library, the auditorium, the lunch room, the audiovisual facilities — are seldom services of value to children under six.

These youngsters are "small towners." They live best in a small world. They need special facilities but their needs are seldom the same as those of their older brothers and sisters. In fact, the time is ripe to look again at our rural areas with the special needs of young children in mind. It is very possible that we ought to reopen our rural one-room schools, where they still exist, or build new modern counterparts. We could use them, dotted all over the countryside, as separate schools for the very young.

The vices and virtues of bigness, however, are not the main urban issue. The depressing impact of low-level homogeneity is. Head Start faces this dilemma. By law, Head Start is an economically segregated program — specifically for poor children. A Head Start group could have an excellent staff, excellent equipment and space. But it commonly lacks one major educational force: heterogeneity. Almost all of the children come from the same disadvantaged background—they learn less from each other. Head Start has the leeway of allowing its groups to enroll 10% to 15% of their children from non-poverty families. Educational parks could make possible an even better mix.

It is too early, however, to consider the case for urban centralization for young children proven one way or the other. Educational parks may be the urban answer. They may also, like our rural central schools, be a better answer for older children than for younger ones. The evidence in favor of trying the idea of educational parks with their heterogeneous mix comes from our depressing experiences with bad ghetto schools and from Head Start. Small class size and ample staffing give Head Start groups the chance to be good; the shortage of skilled teachers, the lack of equipment, the difficulties of financing, as well as low-level homogeneity, have made many less than top-notch. The obstacles have balanced the opportunities. Many groups have been good; few have been excellent; none has been going long enough to give a conclusive answer.

It remains possible that — given excellent staff, facilities, equipment, size — groups for the youngest children can become excellent learning centers, even if they are homogeneous groups economically or racially. Teachers of young children have a real stake in this controversy as it moves along. It will be up to them to make sure that the advantages young children need — smallness, intimacy, the personal touch, the involvement of parents, the freedom to have an active program — are not forgotten.

Meetings of Teachers of Young Children

Lack of organization has contributed to the meekness and silence of teachers of young children. The complaint is nationwide. "Faculty meetings center around older children; the younger ones are never discussed. I feel so all alone." State meetings focus on older children: "Nothing is ever said that relates to the under-six age. I feel so all alone."

It is very difficult for the forgotten minority to speak out.

Some public kindergarten teachers have helped their situation by meeting informally on a city-wide basis. Starting this way, some have managed to achieve an organizational status so that on in-service days they officially meet together. Some have persuaded their state education associations to include kindergarten programs in the annual state meeting. The growth of solidarity has been as important as the new ideas that have come through these meetings. Initially this solidarity meant: *Misery loves company.* Soon spirits rise and a better motto takes over: *In unity there is strength.* A teacher goes back to her own school emboldened by knowing that other teachers are fighting for the same ideas: better class size, more aides, less pressure on reading, more equipment, outdoor space . . . .

Similar moves toward organization have taken place among the teachers of young children in private nursery schools and co-ops and day care centers. There are local affiliates of the National Association for the Education of Young Children and the Association for Childhood Education International all over the country. Often, wisely, these groups draw no line between private school and public school, between nursery school or kindergarten or day care center or Head Start — they include everyone concerned with young children.

> *Every teacher of the young is well-advised to join some early childhood education group, the local ACE or the local NAEYC. Or if no group exists in your community, start one!*

There is need of some counterbalance to the too-prevalent notion that school is school is school.

PARENTS

Pressure from parents is another rough abrasive on programs for young children. Parents are glad their youngsters are going to school, but the "school" they remember best is their own last year of senior high school. Most of today's parents did not go to nursery school or kindergarten. They buy the idea of school for their young children — they think that school is good — but their reasons are not clear: Good for what? What kind of school? And why? Under what conditions?

Youngsters cannot be the school's interpreters. Their answer to the old question — What did you do today? — is well known: "Played." Nor can any one-shot interpretation — one hectic PTA evening, one brief Start-To-School booklet — suffice to build understanding. Halfhearted and half-baked efforts to build understanding are more apt to arouse parents' fears and confusions than to allay them. These efforts seem to indicate that their child was right — they do just play! At least, they certainly move around a lot and there is a lot of noise. "School is not the least bit the way it was when I went to school" . . . in 12th grade!

Parents are buffeted by a steady stream of glib popular magazine articles about early reading, early math, early science . . . . Their anxieties mount: "Teach them something. Teach them something tangible. Teach them something I can grab hold of." Teachers find themselves on the defensive: "We don't teach reading but we do teach reading readiness" . . . "We are getting them ready for first grade" . . . "We are putting on a show for Valentine's Day or Easter or Hallowe'en or Mother's Day or Arbor Day!"

Without active, continuous interpretation by teachers, the classroom becomes less and less right for the children who come; it takes on a design better fitted to older children — the children of many years ago fuzzily in the parents' memories, not the live young children of today.

Ways of Working with Parents

Fortunately there are many well-established ways of working with parents. Countless conscientious and committed teachers have broken the ground and shown how it is possible to win the support of parents for good practices.

The first step is always the same: We have to build good personal relationships with parents. Mothers and fathers must know their child's teacher; you must know the parents. Strangers cannot communicate. Strangers seldom feel trust and confidence. Distance does not lend enchantment; it only breeds suspicion.

Nursery school and day care center teachers have an advantage here. The age of their children and the need for the parent to make some arrangement for the child's enrollment generally necessitate an initial relationship. In Head Start, and especially in the public school kindergarten, nothing automatically brings home and school together in the most effective way. We have to build in machinery. The present practice of one large meeting for all parents, a Spring Roundup, is totally inadequate, and much too impersonal. A parent needs to meet the specific person who will be teaching her child.

Some teachers, sensing the importance of this for future relationships, come on the job early. They give a week or so of their time so that they can visit every parent at home or invite the parent to school. Their goal is simply to chat, to start a relationship so that there is a chance of their becoming friends. Other teachers, not as free to give the time, at least telephone every parent to say "Hello" and to introduce themselves. This is a simple good beginning, an easy gesture of friendliness.

Either approach requires that teachers know ahead of time the names of all of the youngsters they will have in their class. A teacher has a right to insist on this simple administrative service. The start of school for young children cannot be a cold, mechanical, confused, frightening melee: young children lined up in the hall, assigned to teachers arbitrarily at the last minute, an impersonal machine-like shuffling of humans.

The beginning days of school are critically important, too. Even some nursery schools, where the need for personal attention and for warmth is so apparent, make all the children come at once and then bluntly tell the parents: "Go home!" Opening days are exciting, emotion-laden days for parents and children. We have to find ways of living them as sensitively as possible.

Youngsters — nursery school and kindergarten age — feel more comfortable and safe with a staggered start. Parents feel more welcomed with a staggered start. Parents and teachers get a better chance to know each other. Individual children often need their parents with them for the beginning days or longer. Why anyone would deny a young child this comfort is beyond under-standing. But parents need comfort, too. When we say "Go home!" parents do go home . . . rebuffed. Fortunately more and more teachers find it easy to say the more decent words :"Stay! . . . Stay as long as your child needs you . . . I am glad to have you here." And these teachers are glad. The parent has the chance to see a good program in operation. The teacher and the parent have some time to talk.

Even good day care centers, whose mothers frequently are under financial pressure to stay on a job or to find a job, make it clear to parents that they are completely welcome to stay at the start, if they can find a way of doing so. Sometimes parents delay taking a job for a short while until their child is well settled. Sometimes they can make provisions to arrive on the job a little late for a few days to insure that their youngster makes a good beginning.

The telephone is a useful tool, especially at the beginning of the school year. We use it too little, as if it were a new device to be saved for world-shaking messages. If a mother cannot stay — if she is a working mother or has younger children at home or the school's rules may still be slanted anti-parent — a phone call from the teacher at the end of the day brings the parent information she is delighted to have. More important: The phone call conveys the feeling-tone teachers of young children must build: *We* are in this together — the two of us, home and school, friends, partners — we keep in touch, we support each other.

Parent Education

"Parent Education" has gone a little out of style. The words have such a snooty sound. But "parent education" is exactly the right term to describe what a teacher has to do about the happenings in her classroom, now that school is underway. The teacher is there day after day; the parent is not. The teacher knows what goes on; the parent does not. The teacher has the information; the parent does not. There is no reason at all for holding back on educating parents about a school's activities.

We should use every technique we can. The telephone again can play a part. Our room meetings can center on the group's program. Bringing parents into the room as aides and participants, so that they can see with their own two eyes, is obviously an excellent approach. Still another good technique — a very simple one, not used nearly as commonly as it should be — is a Teacher's Newsletter, a weekly or biweekly report to parents. The Newsletter is the teacher's "State of the Union" message but delivered more often than the President gives his. It is analogous to the reports to stockholders on which industry spends millions of dollars, but a Teacher's Newsletter does not have to be on glossy paper or bound or illustrated. It is the simple story of what the children did and why they did it: the books they heard, the songs they sang, the trips they took, the visitors who came, the discussions that went on, the experiments the children tried . . . .

Parents need full information if they are to make constructive judgments about schools. We need the approval of parents. We need their support so that the teacher is not driven into absurdities and is not everlastingly on the defensive. We need parents who will reenforce what the school is doing. We need parents who will supplement what the school is doing.

Our past relationships — our lack of close relationships — have been geared to keeping the peace. We have tried to stay clear of problems. We have kept away from parents on the theory that what they don't know won't hurt them. But in fact ignorance has hurt parents. It has hurt teachers and it has hurt children. We cannot go on this way.

Closer relationships may lead to some temporary outbreak of hostilities. Full and mutual understanding sometimes comes argumentatively, the product of hard and long discussions. No one can say that life is pleasant and cheerful when there are temporary disagreements. But at least we do know that life is healthier when feelings are out in the open. We have learned this with children. We no longer urge them to hide their emotions. Once we know what displeases or worries someone, we stand a chance of doing something about it. And we know from children, too, that problems seldom disappear simply because they are ignored. The whole tendency of problems is to smoulder underground and then to explode. Facing up to problems causes some headaches, but avoiding problems can make us hurt all over.

There is moreover one very reassuring note we must not lose sight of: Most parents are fully prepared to give wholehearted support to good education, once they have the chance to think and talk about it. What parents want for their youngsters is not different from what a good teacher wants. Our task is not the difficult one of "educating" parents to ideas they basically reject. We have the immensely more pleasurable challenge of helping them see how their deepest convictions translate into school practice.

Parents are as sold as any teacher on the worth and importance and dignity of the individual. The individual, after all, is their child.

Parents are as sold as any teacher on the wholeness of humans, on the interrelatedness of social and emotional and physical and intellectual development. A home, after all, does all of these jobs.

Parents know about readiness and motivation, although they may not use these words. They have lived with their children and have had to take these ideas into account.

Parents are sold — almost over-sold — on the idea that experience is the best teacher. They only need help in translating this firmly-held belief into "play" and "trips" and Happenings and other school practices.

Parents know what young children are like. They know their activity. They know their egocentricity. They know their shyness.

They know their noise level and their imagination, their messiness, their sociability . . . Parents have lived with their children since birth. But parents do not always realize that school can be *for* children, not a device to reform them.

Parents hold the same broad goals for their children that teachers do. We are not competitors or opponents pulling in opposite directions. We have been strangers. We operate in different leagues. We have not talked together enough to discover all our common understandings. Our isolation has made it hard for the teacher to be a professional, using all she knows in her classroom. It will take time to close the gap, but it can be done and the effort is worth the while.

Index